PRAISE FOR:
"FINALLY FEARLES_"

"This is one courageous book. In her bravest turn yet, Cheryl McKay dives into the storm-tossed depths of suffocating anxiety. It is a work of faith in its most practical and sometimes harrowing expression. This unflinchingly honest, soul-baring account is the personal hand of experience, reaching out across the churning seas of fear, guiding all who would read to still waters and lasting peace.

— **Susan Rohrer**, author of *THE HOLY SPIRIT: Amazing Power for Everyday People* & *IS GOD SAYING HE'S THE ONE? Hearing from Heaven about That Man in Your Life*

"With courage and an endearing transparency, Cheryl once again opens her life as a tribute to the grace of her Lord. From the valleys of despair to the mountaintops of victory, through the deserts of loneliness to the healing springs of God's personal words to her heart, Cheryl reveals her journey from panic to peace. And in the process, she offers hope and help to those who, like she was for so many years, are bound by fear and panic. She is living proof that our Savior did, indeed, come to set the captives free!"

— **Mark & Patti Virkler,** authors of *4 Keys to Hearing God's Voice* and *Prayers that Heal the Heart*

"For anyone battling fear and anxiety, this book offers hope that healing is possible. Cheryl's honesty and vulnerability about her deepest fears, heartaches, and periods wrestling with God offer comfort to readers that they are not alone. Cheryl understands how anxiety and fear can imprison you, yet also knows firsthand how the Healer can set you free. Her desire for God to use her pain to help those in the midst of their own battle is clear as she encourages readers toward healing by sharing God's Truth, insights she's learned along the way, and practical tips and assignments that have aided her own journey to freedom."

— **Christa Sands**, author of *Learning to Trust Again*

"*Finally Fearless* is an incredible work! It takes you on a journey from a life of complete brokenness and pain to one that's fully restored and healed through the power of the Holy Spirit. Not only does Cheryl tell you what to do to receive your healing, she shows you step-by-step, illustrating with her own real life examples how to make biblical principles work in your heart. Cheryl shares moments of despair in the depths of depression and then gives a clear pathway to hope and healing. Her testimony is powerful! And if you are in a painful place, you will find one who understands you. Those thoughts you don't want anyone to know. The secrets you've kept hidden for years. Cheryl's been there, she knows and she cares. She's written this intensely personal story to give you hope that you, too, can find peace, redemption, and confidence in Christ.

"And if you're one of the few in this world whose life has not been touched by any kind of abuse (physical, sexual, verbal, spiritual) – praise God! But know that there are people in your life right now who have been ravaged by it. Once you read this book, you'll understand more how they're feeling, what they're thinking, and most importantly, how you can help them. I'm excited to see the breakthroughs and life transforming testimonies that I know will come from this. Thank you, Cheryl, for bravely sharing your story with us! God is using it mightily, and I know that many will find release and freedom as they explore these truths and let the Wonderful Counselor heal them completely - spirit, soul and body."

— **Dr. Charity Kayembe**, Communion with God Ministries

Finally Fearless

Journey from Panic to Peace

How Overcoming Anxiety Helped Me Find True Love

By Cheryl McKay

Purple PenWorks

By Cheryl McKay

Never the Bride (screenplay)
Never the Bride a novel (with Rene Gutteridge)
Greetings from the Flipside a novel (with Rene Gutteridge)
Finally the Bride: Finding Hope While Waiting
The Ultimate Gift (screenplay)
The Ultimate Life (screen story)
Novelizations: How to Adapt Scripts Into Novels (with Rene Gutteridge)
Gigi: God's Little Princess DVD (screenplay)
Wild & Wacky, Totally True Bible Stories Series (with Frank Peretti)
Song of Springhill: a love story
Spirit of Springhill: Miners, Wives, Widows, Rescuers & Their Children Tell True Stories of Springhill's Coal Mining Disasters

Coming Soon:
Love's a Stage (with Rene Gutteridge)
O Little Town of Bethany (with Rene Gutteridge)

For those who are
tired of fear
making their worlds smaller

FINALLY FEARLESS: JOURNEY FROM PANIC TO PEACE
HOW OVERCOMING ANXIETY HELPED ME FIND TRUE LOVE

Cover image © Photocreo Bednarek – Fotolia.com
Cover Design by Christopher Price

Materials from "Dream Interpretation" by Herman Riffel, copyright 1993, used by
permission of Destiny Image Publishers, 167 Walnut Bottom Road, Shippensburg,
PA 17257.

Materials from "Freedom From Fear" by Malcolm Smith used by permission of
Malcolm Smith Ministries, TX.

Materials from "Learning to Trust Again" by Christa Sands, used by permission of
Discovery House Publishers, MI.

Materials from "Counseled by God" by Mark & Patti Virkler, used by permission
of Lamad Publishing, NY.

Materials from "Prayers that Heal the Heart" by Mark & Patti Virkler, used by
permission of Bridge-Logos Publishers, FL.

Materials from "Pigs in the Parlor" by Frank & Ida Mae Hammond, used by
permission of Impact Christian Books, Inc.

Materials from "Overcoming Anxiety" by Archibald D. Hart, Ph.D. used by
permission of Archibald D. Hart, Ph.D.

Poem by Chris Stacy, used by permission.

TABLE OF CONTENTS

PART I: THE PANIC

PART II: THE JOURNEY

PART III: THE PEACE

CHAPTER 9:

CHAPTER 10:

CHAPTER 11:

CHAPTER 12:

Appendices

Chapter Notes

Acknowledgments

About the Author

Suggested Reading List

PART I

The Panic

CHAPTER 1
Unmapped Territory:
The Moment Of Panic

When Jesus spoke again to the people, he said, "I am
the light of the world. Whoever follows me will never
walk in darkness, but will have the light of life."
(John 8:12)

I have been working on pieces of this book for years, gathering journal
entries, pulling together insights from my past, jotting them on lined,
notebook pages. Never before now has the urge to write this book hit
me so clearly.

I've been in the darkest season of my life for the past six months.

I thought I was getting married.

I also thought I was finally putting my panic disorder and anxiety
issues behind me. I can't seem to climb out of this deep, dark pit. Yet, I
feel God is prompting, calling to me:

"Write about it. Tell your story."

I wrestle with Him, asking, "Why? Why should I share my story
when I feel so unhealed myself?"

Maybe in telling it, I will find healing. There's only one way to find out.

It's late 2003 as I embark on this journey to pull together the pieces I already started, and to write anew. To make this story whole.

Only I don't have an ending.

Until I get married, I will not be able to test whether or not I'm truly healed of my anxiety disorder. I promise; that will make sense soon enough.

But everything just fell apart.

I've never felt more alone in my life. This natural life. Physical, tangible life. But I've also never felt God's presence this closely. His voice clearer.

Maybe this is the season. Maybe my healing is finally within grasp. Maybe in sharing my story so openly, others with similar problems and challenges can also find healing. Maybe that will make the past twenty plus years of pain worth it.

I don't want anyone else to suffer the way I have.

> *Cheryl's Journal, a short story (2003)*
>
> *When she found herself at the crossroads, she didn't know which road to take. To go left meant running from her feelings, her fears and pain. But the path was so dim, faint, colorless the entire way. There was no light at its end.*
>
> *To go right meant jumping straight into a long stretch of darkness. Mile after mile. There would be fear and trembling with every step. But at the end of the road to the right lived colors, hues, the light.*
>
> *She asked herself, "Which road should I take?"*
>
> *She chose the left. It may have been dim, but at least it wasn't terrifying.*
>
> *For years, she dragged her feet down that road. With each step, she saw nothing of the life she craved. She felt no fear, yet she also felt no joy. Her life was changeless. Predictable. As she looked ahead, the future held more of the*

same — nothing of the life she hoped to reach. The path led her down the dead end road.

She knew she had to turn back and go right, down that road of darkened, unmapped territory.

She traveled back, mile after mile, before she returned to that fork in the road. Then, she chose the right path. It was dark, daunting, lined with fears to face. But if she refused to walk through these shadows, she'd never find the light. That's the hope she held so tightly.

A Small, Small World

Have panic attacks destroyed any of your dreams? Has fear and the experience of anxiety shrunk your world down to a few safe places? Have your fears caused you to modify where you can go, what you're willing to do, whom you're willing to be with? If so, there's good news: you don't have to stay that way. You can seek healing. There is a way to restore your world back to its normal size with the breadth that includes all the treasures life has to offer. If you've been stuck on the dim road where anxiety gives you limitations and few safe places, it's time to choose a different path. Now is the time to choose the path that leads toward the light. For me, that light came through God, Jesus, and the healing balm of the Holy Spirit.

Through this book, I will share my story. I'll share how I let anxiety rule my life, choosing the dim road that held no hope. I'll share how I finally chose to face my fears and walk toward the light no matter how frightening the path was. I was able to change from the road on the left to that road on the right because God held my hand every step of the way, even when I didn't feel it. I hungered badly enough for the kind of peace that only God could provide to walk through storms, refining fire, and every dark place to reach it.

I hope you'll open your heart's door and journey with me. Perhaps together we can change the way you face your anxieties. Wouldn't you love to be on the path towards freedom from the debilitating effects of fear?

An estimated forty million Americans suffer from some form of an anxiety disorder. It's the most common mental condition, yet only one-third receive treatment or help. (1)

Keeping our disorder a secret is destroying our spirits, trapping us in a jail cell barred with panic, fear, and anxiety. It's time to break the silence and reach out for the help that's available. That can only begin when we first admit we have a problem: to ourselves, to other people, to our healing God.

I am not a psychologist or medical doctor. Most of the time I struggled with an anxiety disorder, I had no idea what was wrong with me and felt alone.

Have you ever felt like you are the only one in the world who has this challenge? Have you kept it a secret because you feel like no one will understand? I hid my problem because I didn't know there were forty million others who had it, too! And for at least ten of the twenty years I had an anxiety disorder, I didn't even know what it was called. That is why I decided to write this book. I want you, my readers, to know you are not alone anymore.

Throughout this book, I will share words I believe God has spoken directly to me during prayer or through dreams. God spoke to me in ways that were able to heal my heart and heal me of my anxiety disorder, freeing me from living with panic attacks and irrational fears. If you don't know how to already, I encourage you to learn how you can hear God's voice so you can welcome Him to heal you divinely. If you read any of the books I talk about, put *Dialogue with God* by Mark and Patti Virkler on the top of that stack. (Please note: *Dialogue With God* now has an updated version since I penned this book, called *4 Keys to Hearing God's Voice*. I also recommend *The Holy Spirit: Amazing Power for Everyday People* by Susan Rohrer).

Hearing what God has to say heals us because God is the Wonderful Counselor. When we learn how to hear and discern His voice, He can speak healing and encouragement to our hearts. He can offer comfort and advice. But if we are not listening, we will not hear. And for many of us, it's simply because we don't know how or we've never been taught.

I firmly believe I would have recovered a lot sooner if I had known how to hear God's voice earlier. I know His counsel helps with emotional struggles because I've used this to help with other emotional problems, like depression. I never would have crawled out of that dark hole without God's intervention and words spoken to me. But God wants to talk to all of us, not just me! Don't think of this as some special gift I have. God loves all of His children and wants nothing more than to be in communication with us.

I don't know if panic ever goes away. The only test is living and seeing if you ever have an attack again. Since none of us know the future, it's hard to tell if panic is ever gone from our lives. I can testify that what used to take over my life is now in the background, a distant memory.

However, if panic or anxiety are at the forefront of your life, there are so many different things you can do to walk actively toward the healing God can give you. That walk will be explored throughout this book.

Let's journey together on the path toward healing, toward a life that is fulfilling and free from overwhelming fear. Notice I didn't say anxiety-free, for that would be tough for anyone who breathes.

The First Panic

I had my first anxiety attack when I was twelve years old. I was in the seventh grade, that grade when I talked to boys, even flirted with a few — the cute ones, of course. I was a normal, healthy young woman.

Wasn't I?

One night the Christian school I attended held a lock-in. You know, one of those nights where kids stay up all night playing games, eating Cheese Doodles and Ding Dongs. I had a boyfriend, if you could call him that at age twelve. That boy was frisky! A little too frisky.

Earlier that day at school, he kept counting up how many kisses I owed him that night at the lock-in. By 4:00 p.m., the count grew to over sixty-five kisses.

The lock-in started at 7:00 in the school's gym, which doubled as our church sanctuary on weekends. Perfect setting for a make-out session, right? My so-called boyfriend wanted to escape to an empty Sunday School classroom so he could cash in on the sixty-five plus kisses I owed him. I thought, *Hmm, I like the idea of kissing him.*

But that's when it hit me.

Suddenly, I felt sick. I couldn't breathe normally. I caught the flu. Or was it too many Ding Dongs? Was Jesus punishing me for craving those kisses in a church building? I had no idea what was happening to my body, but there was no way that boy was going to get any kisses out of me that night! (Or any night thereafter. His eyes suddenly flew to one of my best friends. The heartbreak of junior high!)

That moment marked the beginning of what turned into a twenty-year battle with an anxiety disorder. I didn't figure out what happened to me that night until over ten years later. It was the first time I panicked, but it wouldn't be the last.

The Panic Continues...
Two years later.

At the promising age of fourteen, I was destined to be a star of stage and screen. I was cast in a play at a community theater, playing a teen with a chip on her shoulder. (It was not typecasting. I promise!) I had a big-time crush on one of my co-actors. I'll call him Kirk. (That has nothing to do with my childhood obsession with Kirk Cameron when he was the lovable manipulator, Mike Seaver, on *Growing Pains*.)

While developing my acting interests, I wrote plays, short stories, and skits. My best friend, Lisa, and I were preparing a skit for a drama contest at church. Suddenly, in a burst of creativity, I wrote myself a boyfriend into the scene. I fibbed to Kirk and told him another actor bailed on me at the last minute for the contest. I asked him to come to my rescue and take this fictitious actor's place. (Yeah, I connived my way into his heart. Well, maybe only in my active imagination.)

Did Cheryl have the guts to write a kiss into the scene? Not quite. But how exhilarating it was, when cutie Kirk ran onto the stage to rescue me, his *girlfriend* from the downward spiral in which she'd found herself! I loved being rescued by a man who cared deeply about me. Well, he cared deeply about my character, Jovanna. It was high drama, and Kirk was a great actor. We won the contest: our grand prize—a whole bag of M&M's.

Then I found out the ugly, painful truth: Kirk had a real girlfriend. She wasn't scripted on the page like me. He introduced me to her one night during our community theater play.

That was the night my panic returned.

At a young age, I began keeping journals. I will share many entries throughout this book. This is the first entry I wrote about my challenge with anxiety:

> *Cheryl's Journal (February 23, 1986)*
> *I was so nervous, especially after I met Kirk's girlfriend. I was upset. I also threw up between every scene. I missed two scenes because I was outside getting sick. Everyone thought I had the flu.*

Even though I was upset that night, Kirk's girlfriend and I became good friends, and they welcomed me into their fun group. However, when we'd hang out, the strangest thing happened: I would get a flood of bizarre symptoms and throw up for an hour before Kirk would pick me up. The symptoms included breathing fast, hyperventilating, shaking, sweating, and throwing up. I didn't understand what was happening to my body. I wondered, *Is this the flu? Again?*

Kirk always came to get me first because I lived near him. We'd have half an hour alone in the car before we'd get to his girlfriend's house. I seemed especially nervous about being alone with him, even though we weren't dating. After three different weekends of this cycle, I knew I wasn't just randomly catching the flu over and over. I knew something was wrong, but I had no idea what.

I realized I had a trigger that brought this on: boys — not all boys — but boys I liked. I saw this pattern: an unexplainable pattern. I didn't know what it meant or what this problem was called. I had no idea why it was happening.

In retrospect, I was no doubt having panic attacks, but at the time I had never heard of a panic attack or anxiety disorder. No one could tell me what was wrong or why this was happening to me. I felt strange, abnormal, and confused. All I knew to say to those close to me was, "I get so nervous I throw up." I still didn't know this *condition* had a name.

I never told Kirk what was happening to me. How on earth could I explain it? "By the way, Kirk, every time you're coming to get me, I throw up for an hour." How ridiculously embarrassing!

The symptoms didn't stop once I was with him. If we went out for pizza, I always had to leave the table to get sick. One night, I captured this anxiety in my journal:

> *Cheryl's Journal (March 15, 1986)*
> *Tonight, I went out with Kirk, his girlfriend, and their friend Tim. The whole time, I felt like I was gonna get sick. I left the dinner table and calmly said, "I have to go to the bathroom" and I went and threw up. I don't know why, but I was so nervous! No one found out I was sick.*

That last statement, "No one found out," was highly important to me. I knew something about me wasn't right. I strongly believed I'd be laughed at for throwing up during a normal pizza outing. Hiding the problem was my only solution. I never wanted any attention, especially not this way!

I prayed for God to take my weird problem away or at least help me hide the symptoms. That never worked. There were times hiding my problem was impossible. One time, Kirk, his girlfriend, Tim, and I were on our way to an amusement park. The whole way there, I had been fighting a panic attack in the car to the point of dry heaving. No one noticed! (No clue how I hid that!) Sometimes I wouldn't throw up if I didn't eat. That morning I didn't eat on purpose in case I felt sick. If my stomach were empty, I had a better chance of hiding it. But once we got to the park, my body was like, *enough of this fighting! Let me throw up!* And so I did—in front of everyone—right into a bush. Talk about feeling beyond humiliated! I yanked out my usual lie. "It must be the flu! Yeah, again!" I could not tell this guy it was because of him. I went to the first aid center to rest for a while. I couldn't go on rides. I told them to go on without me. Truthfully, I was aching for a reprieve; I had to get away from Kirk.

While lying on a cot at the first-aid center, I pondered how this was the second time Kirk found out I had been sick, the first being the night of our play. I remember thinking, *Oh, no! Kirk knows I threw up. That means the next time I see him I can't be sick. He's going to know something's weird about me if I get sick again!* I put extra pressure on myself right then that guaranteed I'd struggle the next time I saw him. I put the demand in place that said I wasn't allowed to be this way.

I always tried to hide it so that, if I ever needed a cover story—like this particular day—I'd have it. But that card had been played twice now. How would I explain a flu that never goes away if it happened again? If I admitted he was the cause that would have been like admitting I had feelings for him. I didn't want him to know I liked him since he was dating someone else.

I stayed in the first-aid center until my good friend, Jason, showed up. He was a trusted friend who knew of my unnamed, strange problem—he didn't know what it was called either. His presence helped me calm down enough to go on rides the rest of the day.

When Kirk and his girlfriend broke up, I hoped I'd get a chance to date him. (I even had her blessing!)

One night, we were at Jason's birthday party. Jason announced a lady's choice dance. Lionel Ritchie crooned a sappy love song. I marched right up to Kirk and asked if he would like to dance with me. My heart leaped when he said yes.

We breezed onto the dance floor where all my other fourteen and fifteen-year-old friends slow danced with boys they liked. One stanza into the song, waves of nausea came over me. Panic rose inside: the sweating, the breathing, the churning of my stomach. I craved so much to enjoy this special moment. I clenched my whole body, fought so hard to not get sick while ugly words screamed inside my head: *You're trapped. You have to make it through this whole song. You can't run away now. You'll look stupid. Don't get sick!* I didn't have a chance of succeeding with those words undermining my confidence.

And so, I failed.

Miserably!

During the second verse, I ran away from Kirk, ran away from all my so-called normal friends on the dance floor that were perfectly fine dancing with boys. I ran from what I wanted. I bolted to the nearest bathroom and threw up. There are not enough words to express how humiliated I felt. It's one thing to leave a table during dinner to go to the rest room. But to run away in the middle of a dance I asked for — there was no explaining it. Not to me and not to anyone else.

I cried the rest of the night. I couldn't face Kirk because I had no way of explaining what was wrong with me, why being around him made me sick. He was a nice guy who I wasn't even dating. How could I explain it to him when I had no idea what was happening inside of me?

I'll let my journal tell you how I felt:

> *Cheryl's Journal (April 26, 1986)*
> *During the dance, I had to run to the bathroom to get sick. I was furious at myself. Why do I act so stupidly? We were just dancing. Was anyone else running away? Did*

anyone else look as stupid as I looked? No. I am the only one in the entire world with this ridiculous, stupid, stupid problem.

There were no answers. That entry encapsulates how I felt most of my adolescent life. I had no clue why I was so abnormal. I convinced myself that no other human in the universe had the problem I had. No matter how many times it happened, I never got used to it. I also did not travel any closer to finding an answer to why I had this ugly, embarrassing curse ruining my life. Anger started to boil in me. My closest friends asked, "Why can't you just relax?" I wondered the same thing. In my mind I would tell myself to calm down, but my body never listened. I craved to have a boyfriend, like my other friends, but something kept getting in the way.

I also ached to be more like my older sister, Heather, who was so relaxed and confident around guys. She always had a boyfriend, always knew how to have fun. She seemed fearless; I spent years wondering why I couldn't have been more like her.

I backed off hanging out with Kirk. After he'd seen me get sick three times, I couldn't deal with the risk it would happen again. Then he moved away and the friendship died off. It was a relief more than a loss.

After Kirk left, another boy caught my attention. But the same cycle continued: the nerves, the vomiting, the need to get away. I reached a point where I was tired of hating myself for having these reactions; I decided it wasn't worth liking boys anymore. Who wouldn't grow tired of the humiliation? If I stopped myself from liking boys, I could appear normal to the rest of the world. That seemed like the best solution. Who needs a boyfriend, right?

Running Away
Was running away a long-term solution? As a fourteen-year-old, avoiding dating so I could feel normal wasn't going to hurt me too

much. I could focus on school, cheerleading, community theater, creative writing. (That year, I'd written ten full-length plays, plus a gazillion stories!) I didn't feel like I was missing too much when I chose to avoid liking boys. At least, that's the lie I kept feeding myself. (Instead of dating anyone, I lived vicariously through the teen characters in *Sweet Dreams Romance* books and the characters I wrote into my scripts.)

I chose to walk to the left, down the dimly lit path, the road that avoided fear but did not lead to life. I was not on the path that could bring light into my world. I stayed where it was safe, yet so dark.

My world got smaller because I made the choice to avoid dating. That choice affected my life for many years. While a teenager's life may benefit from avoiding the dating scene, my reasons for avoidance were not healthy. I was driven by fear, a fear I didn't even understand, a fear that I couldn't pull out by its roots because I had no idea where it came from. I wasn't facing my fears because I had no idea how to do that.

A common coping mechanism for those with anxiety is to avoid all situations where panic or anxiety can happen. Did my solution to avoid boys work? Temporarily, yes. My panic attacks went away. But I did come to a point where I knew I would never marry and have a family of my own if I didn't do something about my problem.

What's Your Story?

Has your world shrunk? Have you found yourself avoiding situations that bring on an attack? Have you given up something you want because of the way your body and mind panic over it?

Over the years, I've come across a few women who have this same trigger as the cause of their anxiety attacks: men, dating, and social situations. However, it's not the only reason or even the most common reason people have anxiety disorders.

What scares you? Do you hate driving on the freeway? Do symptoms show up every time you start the car engine? Do you hate waiting in lines at the grocery store or sitting tucked away in a booth at a restaurant? Do you avoid all situations that make you feel trapped? Perhaps you fear animals, heights, water, storms, elevators, talking to people, going to parties, or walking outside. Anytime you think of getting into a situation where you may need to face your fears, your throat closes up, the sweating begins, and your stomach churns. For me, it just happened to be dating. There are countless triggers to this disorder.

I believe that you can learn a lot about how to battle anxiety and rise above it through my story. I think we have a lot in common: our thoughts, our coping methods, the dysfunctional ways we avoid fears. No matter what your particular trigger is, we can all relate to one another because of what we've been through. It seems we're all afraid of something to an extent that goes beyond reason; we have an irrational level of fear that brings with it a flood of symptoms.

The Dreaded Symptoms

The symptoms that overpower us during an attack vary widely. For me, the number one symptom was vomiting. That was the sign of the end of a panic attack. It was almost a relief when I finally stopped fighting it and let myself get sick. I'd get a little reprieve before it would start all over. Before I'd reach the point of throwing up, my throat would tighten, I'd have that smothered feeling, sweaty palms, hot and cold chills, overall nausea, headaches, extreme tightness in my neck and shoulders, pains in my chest. I'd breathe too fast which caused light-headedness and dizziness. There are countless other symptoms.

Malcolm Smith in *Freedom from Fear* describes panic as "the unleashing of fear and anxiety in an overwhelming flood of terror. It produces immobility of the mind, terror in the emotions, sweaty palms, palpitating heart, ringing ears, dizziness, nausea, the feeling that we are on the verge of insanity, hot flashes, chills, choking, and intense loneliness." (1)

Let's get in touch with your personal situation. There is an accompanying workbook available in paperback for this book (*Finally Fearless Workbook*). I hope you'll get it and actively participate in your own healing by doing the assignments throughout this book. (This includes the same assignments I did to work on my own healing. The workbook also contains bonus material and additional exercises.)

> **ASSIGNMENT:**
> **LIST YOUR ANXIETY SYMPTOMS:**
> **Right before a full-blown attack:**
> **During a full-blown attack:**

It's a Heart Thing

We've discussed what the moment of panic is like, the flood of symptoms it brings. Before we get into defining anxiety disorders in the next chapter, I'd like to introduce you to how heart healing can happen, a concept which will track throughout the rest of this book.

Simply put, anxiety, panic, and fear are heart problems; therefore, our hearts must be healed.

Has anyone in your life—with the intent of being helpful—told you during an attack to just relax? My suspicion is that did nothing for your anxiety. I used to want to smack anyone who said that to me! My sarcasm wanted to spew, "Thanks for the advice. Why didn't I think of that?" The irony is, I did think of that, over and over in my mind as it screamed the demand to calm down. There is a great reason that method fails, whether it comes from within or is given by well-intentioned, yet clueless, others. The reason these commands to relax don't work is that anxiety problems find their roots in our hearts. It's rare for the problem to be 100% chemical. It's often an emotional problem. Therefore, we must use a language the heart understands to combat a heart problem. Using rational thoughts and words will never work because it's not a problem that is rooted in the rational side of our being. Mark and Patti Virkler discuss this issue in their book *Prayers that Heal the Heart*. They say, "It is only God's voice, vision and anointing which heal the heart." (2)

Being able to talk to God and to let God counsel you is vital to your ability to heal.

When we are in the midst of an attack, we get caught up in our emotions. Therefore, using rational thought (or left brain functions) will not have any affect on our hearts. We need to use right-brain functions, languages that speak to our hearts, during the onset of an attack. We can go back and think about what happened to us rationally after that attack is over. But in the middle of it, no amount of reasoning will pull us out of it.

I will go into helpful techniques in Chapter 9. Much of what I will suggest uses languages that speak to our hearts. Ironically, the same languages (like visualization and meditation) are used to hear God's voice.

To follow is an excerpt from the Virklers's *Prayers that Heal the Heart* seminar guide, which explains this heart language concept:

1. The heart speaks in a language that is different from that of the mind. Today's society considers the language of the mind to be logical ideas. The Bible considers the language of the heart to be pictures, emotions, flow and faith.

2. Heart healing must occur on the level of the heart, not merely in the mind. To heal the heart **we must use the language of the heart.**

The heart speaks using a language that is different from that of the mind.

Mental reasoning is when one reasons alone and does not merge reason with faith and revelation from the Holy Spirit. In each of the following verses, reason alone was rebuked by Jesus as being ineffective. (Matt.

16:5 — 12, Mk. 2:5 — 12, 8:15 — 18). The result of using reason alone is vanity or meaninglessness (Eccl. 12:8). In today's culture, we would consider reason to be the language of the mind. At the very least, biblically speaking, "reason" is an ineffective language of the heart.

To summarize, effective languages of the heart include: God's divine flow/spontaneity, imagination/pictures/vision, dreams, emotions, godly emotions like love, joy and peace, and pondering/meditation. (3)

Ecclesiastes 11:10 says, "So then, banish anxiety from your heart and cast off the troubles of your body." Notice that even in the Bible, anxiety is referenced as being in *the heart*. We can't banish anxiety with our head alone. We can't tell it to go away and expect it to listen. Therefore, to deal with our fears, we need to deal with the heart. Notice the verse also addresses the way our troubles can live in our bodies.

In the Virklers's book *Counseled by God*, they state, "You can't talk yourself out of fear intellectually because it is not mental but spiritual at its roots. Faith must well up from within you as a result of an encounter with Jesus Christ in order to be set free from fear." (4)

Did I know all of this while I was trying to recover? No! That's why I floundered for twenty years, wondering why yelling at myself to "just stop it" didn't work. I wish I'd known how to deal with my emotional heart back when I was battling all of this. I had to fail a lot before I came to a place that finally brought healing into my heart.

Road that Leads to Healing

I'm sure many of you can relate to feeling low during the moment of panic, feeling that no one cares or understands, feeling like you've exhausted every possible resource for help. I'm here to say there's more to do. That is what this book is about: walking down the road toward healing, allowing God to heal our hearts. That road will not always be easy. In fact, it will be hard. Sometimes scary; sometimes frightening. You've got to travel down this road to make it to the light.

I chose to run away from the light for such a long time. I hope you won't.

Going through the lows is worth it; you will get to the highs. Then, we can move from panic to peace.

Let's continue this journey together.

CHAPTER 2

Rough Terrain:
Anxiety Disorders

The worst fear is the fear of living.
(Theodore Roosevelt)

My hair. Ugh, I hate my hair, I thought, as I stared at my image in the bathroom mirror, getting ready to go out. *Will he like these jeans? This shirt? Is purple a good color for me?* The phone rings. *I bet he's calling to cancel. He must be. Oh. The phone is not for me. Guess he's on his way. Maybe it would be better if he did cancel. He's gonna want to go out to eat. I'm so nauseated. I can't breathe the smell of food, let alone eat it! What am I gonna do? Maybe I'll tell him I already ate. He'll think that's so dumb, considering we had plans to go out. I'm not even remotely hungry. Even though I haven't eaten since… hmm…when was that? Yesterday, I think. He can sit there and eat. I'll just watch. Hope I don't get sick. Get sick. Oh, no. It's coming. Why am I sweating so much? Air. What is happening to the air? I can't get enough. I know! I'll breathe harder. Faster. Yeah, that'll work. Get more air into those lungs. Inhale, exhale. Inhale, exhale. Faster. Faster. I think I'm gonna pass out. Oh, no! Here it comes. I have to throw up!*

Sigh. What is wrong with me? Why do I do this every time? I'm so stupid. No one else gets sick every time they're getting ready for a date. No one else behaves as ridiculously as I do. Why am I like this? I hate myself. If he finds out about this, he'll hate me, too.

The doorbell rings. *Oh no. It's him. How am I gonna do this? I can't go. I'll just have to cancel. I should just give up trying to be like everyone else. I should give up dating.*

Because that scene was beyond typical for me before every date, I spent from late 1986 to the end of 1989 focusing solely on my new dreams: writing and acting. I loved investing myself in the stories of my characters, whether I penned their moves or acted out their emotional journeys. These two new loves became my best friends.

However, during that time, anxiety latched onto one of them. Panic found a new outlet in which to express herself: stage fright. My dream of becoming an actress began when I was eleven. While I fought nerves before my performances, I never had panic attacks during shows until I took on a dramatic role in an AIDS awareness play called *Innocent Man*. I played Jessie, the girlfriend of a guy named Josh, who finds out he's HIV+. I gave her my favorite name and created her character with slices of myself, as it was an unscripted, improvised show. I wrote my own dialogue, reactions, and feelings.

It's amazing I got the part because I was not good! I could only handle being dramatic in the comfort of my own bedroom. On stage, I froze. I couldn't get in touch with my emotions. Even though I wished many times I could cry while playing Jessie, the tears wouldn't come. This mirrored my real life. I had so much control in public that I was unable to release that control and be vulnerable onstage, even though it was just acting.

I feel it is no coincidence the show that caused the most panic attacks was this particular AIDS story. This drama had loss and fears of loss at its heart. Also, intimacy between this young woman and her boyfriend was a hot topic of discussion because of her need for an AIDS test. Jessie also felt rejected because Josh contracted his disease from a previous girlfriend he loved, even more than Jessie herself. These themes resonated with me on a deeper level than I realized at the time. As a result, panic came back into my life without me even dating anyone offstage.

Our drama troupe did two shows a day in junior high schools. I'd get sick before and between shows. I became known as the cast member who never ate lunch with the rest of them, yet another way of highlighting my abnormalities. In fact, at the end of the run of the show, during our fake Oscar-style awards night, I won an award tailored just for me: it was called "most festive eating habits." No one realized how big my problem was. They poked fun, which was fine with me! I never wanted anyone to know my problem was a lot more serious than regular stage fright.

After that show, I resorted to bit parts and chorus roles so I could still work in theater without being in the spotlight. (I was that rare actress who didn't want attention.)

Because I was so locked emotionally, I was unable to shine onstage. My emotional and anxiety problems—again—were stomping on my dreams. But I had no idea how to fix myself.

Ultimately, my well-meaning acting teachers told me not to bother chasing that dream. I understand why they felt I shouldn't. Actors need to be open, vulnerable, and free with emotions. I had none of these working in my favor.

Are you seeing a pattern here? Anxiety had more control over my life than I did.

Off the Deep End

Near the end of 1989, I was on the brink of adulthood, about to turn eighteen years old. I felt I had matured a lot during those three loveless, dateless, crush-free years. So, when a particular guy—I'll call him Greg—caught my attention, I wanted to try dating again. He worked at the same movie theater I did. He caught my eye by showing an interest in me first. Believe me when I say that was a rare occasion! (I learned later in my life that I gave off a strong, fearful "stay away from me" vibe that discouraged most guys from asking me out.) His overt interest also gave me a lesser chance of rejection! It didn't take long for me to get hooked. He was a Christian, adorable, fun, responsible, yet also a dreamer, a creative guy who was going places. (And, boy, did I want to go where he was going!) He was twenty-one years old. I really liked this guy! My desire to be his girlfriend gave me the courage to go for it! Surely, that little problem with nerves I had as a mere child had disappeared by now, right? I wanted to be right.

I was wrong.

As soon as we started dating, anxiety plagued my life in full force. The panic attacks returned with their many symptoms and continuous vomiting.

Again, I chose to keep my problem a secret. I liked Greg too much to "burden him" with my unusual problem. I believed no guy could accept an imperfect *me*, the *me* who struggled. I believed guys would only choose women who didn't have problems.

Here is where I used my unhealthy coping mechanism. You know, the one where I had more control over the appearance of my anxiety if I hadn't eaten. Even if I still felt nauseated, I didn't have to run to the bathroom as often if my stomach were empty. I even learned how to gag in someone's presence and make it look like I was laughing. I know! It sounds impossible, but I had lots of practice. The only way it worked was if I didn't eat the entire day I'd see Greg. I still went through the rest of the other symptoms before I'd see him. I could hide those a lot better if my stomach weren't trying to reject what I'd just eaten.

This was no solution. With Greg, I lost too much weight. At 5'7", I was usually a healthy 125 pounds. Within weeks of dating him, I dropped to 109. I tried to hide how bad I looked under baggy clothes.

One day, when Greg found out I'd been getting sick, I didn't want to tell him that he was the cause. Instead, I made up the name of my disorder. I said, "Greg, I'm an involuntary anorexic." What's an involuntary anorexic? I have no idea either. Why was that less embarrassing to me than admitting my problem with nerves? Who knows! He looked at me, dumbfounded, and said, "You are not anorexic." I tried to explain that what was wrong with me was like being anorexic, but I'm not choosing to be. I wasn't trying to lose weight, but I was. He didn't buy that excuse any more than I did. I had no logical explanation to offer. I continued to go out with him, never eating in his presence.

And then it happened: I landed in the hospital.

Have you ever found yourself between the pasty white, drab, sterile walls of a medical facility? Have you sat on the cot in the ER shaking, questioning why you're having a heart attack at your ripe, young age? Has the person who checked you out ever said to you, "There's nothing wrong with you"? If so, did you smack them? I wanted to!

One night, I had plans to see Greg. But there was one problem: I couldn't breathe. My chest hurt so badly; it was tightening. I could barely walk, let alone speak. My parents were out of town, so my friends, Lisa and Deanna, were staying with me. They got so worried about my inability to get oxygen that they demanded I let them take me to the hospital. After much protesting on my part, I finally relented.

And so we went.

I go in for the chest X-ray. The doctor tells me his annoying diagnosis: "There's nothing wrong with you." *Excuse me? I'm experiencing this much pain and you say nothing is wrong?* I was fuming, beyond embarrassed. Dr. Annoying did ask me an interesting question: "Are you under any abnormal stress or anxiety?" I thought, *what a bizarre question!* I lied, told him no. But in my mind, I thought, *I do have a new boyfriend.* But how on earth was I supposed to tell that to the doctor in the emergency room? How stupid could I be? It was the first time someone asked me if my symptoms related to anxiety. But did I wake up and realize that I had an anxiety disorder? No. I still had never heard that term. While I told Greg I had to go the hospital, he had no idea it had something to do with him.

The movie theater where we worked offered Greg a promotion if he'd be willing to move away. I felt devastated when he told me he had this big decision to make. I raged inside with angry thoughts: *Of course, something good is finally happening to me, and it's getting ripped away. Nothing good ever stays in my life. Everyone always leaves.* I was consumed with a fear of abandonment. I felt any time I chose to care about someone he'd leave or get taken away. I felt this situation was about to prove my fears correct.

Ultimately, Greg decided not to take the promotion so he wouldn't have to move away from his family and friends — and me. Yes, he told me that I was why he wanted to stay. He also wrote a beautiful letter in which he revealed that he loved me. He was the first man to ever write those words in a note to me. He didn't say it, but it mattered to me that he wrote them down. Wow. Someone loved me? I couldn't believe it. If I'd known how to love someone at that stage of my life, I would have loved him. I felt attached to him and cared deeply about him. I don't think I knew how to love someone though; at least not in the sacrificial, unconditional way maturity brings to a relationship. But this decision on his part settled my anxiety. I grew to feel comfortable with him, like I belonged with this guy. I even began to eat around him.

But that's when he broke up with me.

One month after he decided to stay in town supposedly for me and wrote the words, "I love you."

Should I mention this break up was a few days before Valentine's Day?

I was devastated, left with a mistrust for men and the words they say. I know Greg grew tired of my need for assurance. My insecurity was unattractive; I wanted more attention than he could give me. While I understand now why he walked away, I felt like I was never going to be worth the trouble for any guy. How would I ever find a man who would treasure me enough to stick around? I didn't think any man would ever choose me or love me.

I knew whatever problem I had was ruining my life and relationships. I was living what seemed like a self-inflicted nightmare, but I didn't know how to wake myself up.

A Slammed Door

After the relationship with Greg ended, I stayed away from any guys I liked for years. I dated one guy I didn't care much about because it was the only way to date without panic attacks. I believe I was panic-free because there was little at stake. My heart wasn't involved. (Yes, I was the jerk of that relationship.) Other than that one relationship, for over five years I refused to like anyone, refused to date anyone I could potentially like. For a long time, I believed I was alone, the only one in the whole world with this unnamed problem.

This Problem has a Name

When I was twenty-one, almost ten years after my first anxiety attack, I still had never been diagnosed, still hadn't seen a counselor. So, how did I finally find out I was having panic attacks?

When I was in grad school in 1993 at Regent University, I came across old episodes of a spin-off of *The 700 Club*. It was called *Heart to Heart with Sheila Walsh*. Sheila had Christian music artist, Michael English, on her show. He was discussing his struggles with a panic disorder. When I heard him describe his struggles—the sudden nature of a flood of symptoms coming out of nowhere—I was fascinated with him. His experience sounded so familiar. I looked up articles on him at the library to get more information. I had never heard someone talk about panic before. I thought, *Wow! I wonder if this is what I have.* The more I read about Michael and his struggles, the more I became convinced that I had some kind of an anxiety disorder.

So, did I get help then? Are you kidding? I was in grad school, getting a 4.0, working two jobs, doing lots of film and writing projects, having a great time. A great time not dating! All I had to do was not date, and I would be fine. Michael English's story intrigued me, but it did not drive me to seek help.

Monster of the Mind

CBS's *48 Hours* — hosted by Dan Rather — did a show about this panic that holds us captive, and subtitled it, *Monster of the Mind*. Appropriate, isn't it? They discussed how millions of Americans suffer from some form of an anxiety disorder. Still think you're alone? I'm surprised that since so many other people share this problem, I hardly ever heard anyone talk about it. In truth, others in my life did share this problem; they just weren't talking about it either.

Our embarrassment over having this problem is what keeps us silent. It's a silence we must break. I'll speak more about breaking that silence in Chapter 8.

Does all of this sound familiar to you? Are you certain you have an anxiety disorder? Have you been diagnosed? I urge you to reach out and get help to find out for sure.

> **ASSIGNMENT:**
> Take out your journal or *Finally Fearless Workbook* and write down the answers to the following: **What are you avoiding? What causes you to panic? List every person, place, or thing that triggers panic reactions in you.**

To follow is a journal entry I wrote after I found out through a written test that my problem was indeed an anxiety disorder. It was twelve years after my first panic attack:

Cheryl's Journal (April 1996)
We went over the results of my psychological test. I scored 100% probability on having an anxiety disorder. No

surprise there. I also scored high on avoidant behavior. The test even pinpointed my extreme fear of abandonment. It's amazing how accurate these things are! It also said I have a mild case of depression. It said my problems come out in physical ways because I won't allow them to come out normally through my emotions. Apparently, I'm afraid of my emotions, afraid I won't be accepted for showing them and being honest about them. Sometimes, I end up resenting the person who I perceive causes me to close up. All of this depresses me because it makes me feel like the road ahead of me just got longer. Apparently, I use anxiety for a purpose, probably to hide my feelings. It keeps me from showing my real emotions. I know that's true in relationships because they involve showing emotion and talking about serious issues. I use anxiety to protect myself from getting too close. I need to let that go and replace it with something else. But, what? The opposite is to let myself be who I am and feel and show emotions. But how do I do that? How do I let myself be that vulnerable? Ironically, the test also showed that I harbor resentment because of past hurts I never had the chance to talk about or confront. How on earth can these tests be so accurate?"

Anxiety Disorders Defined

Panic invades our lives, uninvited, unwelcome, like a houseguest that refuses to leave.

How would you define anxiety? What words come to mind when you think of panic? Frightening, debilitating, consuming—hardly anything I want to welcome into my life. I won't go in-depth defining what it is. There are many other books that do that, and you've probably already read them. I will just share a few pieces from the experts. For anyone who's unsure of whether this is your problem, this overview may help you determine if it's worth seeking more information.

Webster's defines panic as "a sudden, unreasoning, hysterical fear, often spreading quickly." Anxiety is "a state of being uneasy, apprehensive, or worried about what may happen... an abnormal state like this, characterized by a feeling of being powerless and unable to cope with threatening events, typically imaginary, and by physical tension, as shown by sweating, trembling." (1)

"Typically imaginary."

What do those words stir up in you? They make me mad! Do they also frustrate you, to think that what we're anxious about is usually an imaginary situation? It's the scenario we've run through our heads that might happen, but usually the chances are slim. Yet, we react as though it's a sure thing. Sometimes, we even "make" it happen with our thoughts.

The various types of anxiety disorders are panic disorder, social and simple phobias, generalized anxiety disorder, obsessive-compulsive disorder, post-traumatic stress disorder, and agoraphobia.

Fear by Association

Panic may start in one territory of our lives, but it quickly takes over other areas. On the *48 Hours* special with Dan Rather, Donny Osmond discussed his battle with an anxiety disorder. He mentioned that he even got nervous seeing his therapist who helped him overcome panic because he associated her with the period of time he battled his disorder.

It doesn't take much for panic to spread like a bad virus. For me, I first panicked over a particular boyfriend. That influenced me to stop dating altogether. But the spread didn't stop there! Because I'd panicked in restaurants, I started to fear them. If I could manage to go inside, I had to sit at a table, not at a booth; I had to be free to run away. Then church pews started to remind me of restaurant booths. I could no longer sit in one unless I sat on the end.

I hated being a passenger in a car or in line at a grocery store because they made me feel trapped. Can you wait in line with a full cart, only to abandon the perishables as you run out of the store? Well, you can, but telling yourself you can't kills your ability to feel the freedom you have. It seems like whatever makes us panic first is no longer our only trigger. It may have started with a particular object, person, or activity. But soon, we find it branching out to many objects, people, or activities.

Fear of Fear

The other way panic spreads is through what's known as the *fear of fear*. Dr. Hart, in *Overcoming Anxiety*, explains, "Perhaps the most complicating factor of all in managing panic disorder is that the experience of a panic attack can be so frightening, even to the strongest and most resilient among us, that it sets up its own cycle of anxiety. In other words, the sufferer becomes so afraid of re-experiencing the panic attack that this fear itself becomes the source of further anxiety. This is known as the 'fear of fear' reaction." (2)

Have your fears made you run away from what you want? Have they interfered with the hopes or dreams you have for your life? For me, they did for years! Of course I wanted love in my life, but I wanted the panic and all its symptoms gone more. I sacrificed relationships that could lead to love so I could have my so-called safety.

Panic: Our Protector?

What is your anxiety disorder protecting you from? It tends to develop as a defense mechanism. Our bodies are trying to protect ourselves from what we perceive to be dangerous. Our job (and one of the main goals of this book) is to figure out what that is.

Our bodies turn on their emergency responses, even though we're not in danger. Perhaps together we can figure out where this problem came from and what we truly fear. That was the number one question I set out to answer; it took me twenty years to find it, then overcome it. I hope you won't flounder in the dark as long as I did.

ASSIGNMENT:

Write in your journal a list of all possible events, people, circumstances, emotions, and objects that anxiety may be trying to protect you from. (Examples from my list include: to keep from getting hurt, rejected, abandoned, and protection from being too intimate with someone or opening my heart.) Brainstorm everything you can think of that you may consider to be a physical or emotional danger to you, whether it actually is dangerous or not.

Chemical or Emotional?

If you've officially been diagnosed as having an anxiety disorder, has your doctor told you if your problem is chemical, emotional, or both? It's rare to find a disorder that is all chemical. Most of us with this problem need to journey toward healing our hearts. A heart full of fear is a heart that needs healing, not just a prescription that will numb those fears. While many people do not have the option of being med-free, I believe you can benefit by doing the heart-work outlined in this book that can bring forth your emotional healing.

I did use medication for a short time, and I will share that part of my journey in Chapter 9. For a long time, I refused to even consider it. I feared getting dependent on meds. I just knew my problem was rooted in something emotional. I wanted to deal with the problem that way, instead of just taking medication. But you know what? Avoidance became my medication. Really, that is no different. There were times in the midst of many panic attacks when it was beyond ridiculous that I wouldn't take them. I was too hard on myself. Please know that I understand there are people who don't have a choice. Some of you may need medication to function. There is nothing wrong with that; and one should never take or stop taking medication without supervision of a doctor.

If medication masks your symptoms so much that you don't even feel like you have a problem anymore, don't use that as a reason to not work on your emotional well-being. We need a healing no medicine can reach. Since fear is not from God, fear should be dealt with, not just numbed. We need to invite God to come in and do a good work in us, to heal us.

Panic — Biblically Defined

Considering the volume of material in the Bible devoted to such commands as "fear not" and "trust God," this must have been something people struggled with a lot. We are not a unique generation. Clearly, God knew this would be an ongoing issue for generations. Recognize that you are not alone. People in the Bible panicked or allowed fears or a lack of faith in God to drive their actions as well.

Think of Adam and Eve, who, as soon as they sinned for the first time, hid from God. That was the beginning of fear in the Bible (Genesis 3).

Think of Abraham and Sarah, who feared they would never have an heir. Their lack of trust in God drove them to take action into their own hands, which resulted in Ishmael's conception (Genesis 16).

Think of Moses, who kept asking, "Who am I," citing his many personal inadequacies to lead the Israelites. When God turned Moses's rod into a snake, Moses ran in fear (Exodus 4:3). Moses feared public speaking (Exodus 4:10). Moses begged God to use someone else, letting his insecurities overpower him (Exodus 4:13). Doesn't Moses sound like a man with an anxiety disorder?

Think of Gideon, who feared his limits and doubted his abilities. He questioned if God was going to help him. He was afraid God had abandoned him and the Israelites (Judges 6:13). God counseled Gideon with the words, "Peace! Do not be afraid. You are not going to die" (Judges 6:23). Then Gideon built an altar and named it "The Lord is Peace" (Judges 6:24). Gideon had the right reaction and became a man of faith. God's counsel sunk into Gideon's heart.

Think of David, who attempted to cover up his sin with Bathsheba by arranging the murder of her husband Uriah. David feared the consequences he'd have to face if his sin came to light. It drove him deeper into sinful behavior (2 Samuel 11).

Think of Elijah, who after working so closely with God to take down Baal and his prophets, ran, fearing for his life after Jezebel threatened him (1 Kings 18–19).

Think of Jeremiah, who cried out to God, "I do not know how to speak; I am only a child" when God told him He'd appointed Jeremiah to be a prophet to the nations (Jeremiah 1:5–6). He was afraid of the work God had for him.

Think of Peter, when he stepped out of the boat; he was fine until he took his eyes off Jesus. Then, he saw the waves around him and panicked (Matthew 14:22–33). And let's not forget when Peter feared for his life and denied Christ three times, running away from the courtyard (Matthew 26:69–75).

Some of these illustrations of people from the Bible were legitimate situations to feel fear or panic (unlike most anxiety disorder situations). However, they still illustrate that big reactions to fear have been around for a long time. Our loving God cared enough to leave us these stories about people we can relate to, along with hundreds of verses encouraging us to trust God, not to live in fear. Our fear must be replaced with faith. But how do we do that?

Our Lord, Our Healer

God is a God of peace, not fear. If we are experiencing fear, we are letting something grip us that is not from God. The Devil is the author of fear and anxiety. Therefore, we need to battle fear in the spirit realm with God's help and armor. Considering 2 Thessalonians 3:16 (kjv) says, "Now the Lord of peace himself give you peace always by all means," this must mean we have access to this *always*. There must be a way to get rid of anxiety. If we have anxiety, it's something we need to pray through and ask God to help us.

In *Counseled by God*, the Virklers state, "Probably the most paralyzing emotion which can overwhelm us is fear. No other emotion can so effectively negate our faith, stifle our joy, disrupt our peace and [handcuff] our walk with the Lord.... Jesus came to heal us of our fear.... Only a living encounter with Christ can transform your heart of fear to a heart of faith.... Jesus is the Counselor Who can destroy the debilitating fear which consumes us and ignite again the faith we need to live a life of victory." (3)

That sums it up, right there. It's what we need to heal from our anxiety disorders. No amount of counseling, self-help books, or medication alone can heal you. This is a problem that needs to be taken to Jesus, our Divine Healer.

Isaiah 26:3 says, "You will keep in perfect peace those whose minds are steadfast because they trust in you."

It's so important when dealing with fears and anxieties that our minds actively pursue God. Our minds won't naturally stay steadfast. We need to listen to God's calming voice or it can be overpowered by the voice of the devil. And boy, does the enemy love to plant those seeds of fear and doubt in us! Notice we also have the responsibility to trust God.

When we get into Part II of this book—The Journey—and Part III—The Peace, I will discuss the ways God counseled me toward emotional wellness. To benefit from this book, your heart needs to be open to Jesus stepping in and helping you through this healing process. And it is a process! None of this will happen overnight.

In the next chapter, I will outline the many traits those of us with anxiety problems have in common. You'll discover even more ways that you are not alone.

Just remember! God is so much stronger than any fears we have. John 16:33 reminds, "I have told you these things, so that in me you may have peace. In the world you will have trouble. But take heart! I have overcome the world."

CHAPTER 3

Stormy Waters:
Do We Sail Alone?

We also glory in our sufferings, because we know that
suffering produces perseverance; perseverance,
character; and character, hope. And hope does not put
us to shame, because God's love has been poured out
into our hearts through the Holy Spirit, who has been
given to us.
(Romans 5:3–5)

Has God ever given you a picture of your life in a dream? Many times,
God has counseled me through dreams by giving me a snapshot of the
condition of my heart. One night, He gave me a dream that contained
an accurate picture of where I was in my life because of my fears:

> *I was on a large boat. Alone. I could hear people having*
> *fun on the deck above, but I chose to be inside the lower level*
> *where it was safer, glassed in.*
>
> *Outside the window, I saw tsunamis. Other boats were*
> *trying to outrun these tall waves, almost as if they were*
> *surfing. They'd ride in front of the rippling wave, fight to*
> *stay afloat, then turn around and catch another one. As I*
> *watched through a glass window, I thought,* they're crazy!
> They could get hurt or drown if they hit a wave wrong!

As I continued to watch their craziness, I realized that despite the danger, they all remained unharmed. Plus, they enjoyed a great adventure, thriving on that risk. In other words, they were living while I remained protected inside, not having any fun.

This dream showed that I was staying away from what scared me, watching the rest of the world enjoy what I was too afraid to do.

I always learn from my dreams. I pay close attention to them because I strongly believe God counsels through them today just as He did so often throughout the Bible. I'll discuss more about dreams in Chapter 9.

Our Common Bonds
Do we sail alone?

Have I mentioned anxiety disorders are the most common mental problem? A quick Internet search will yield a list of famous people who've struggled. The more I read about panic and people who suffer, the more I realize we are not alone. I've found that many of us have similar personality traits—both positive and challenging—that contribute to our problem. Many of us are:

Intelligent
Creative
Perfectionists
Insecure with low self–esteem
Control freaks
Depressed
Afraid of the same things

Dr. Hart in *Overcoming Anxiety* makes an interesting observation. "Anxiety is often assumed to be a sign of spiritual or psychological weakness, but nothing could be further from the truth! Very often, those who suffer from a sudden and incapacitating attack of anxiety are competent, responsible, and normally healthy individuals. This may be part of the problem, in fact. Because they *are* competent and able to do so much, they tend to be highly driven, deeply committed, and overly *stretched* people." (1)

Let's discuss our commonalities.

We're Intelligent

This is good news, right? Most of us are intelligent. Personally, I like being intelligent (although I hardly liked my "Brainiac" nickname in junior high school). We may use the left side of our brains more often than our right—the left is where rationalization and reasoning live. But who said anxiety disorders are rational? They're not, which is why we can't stay on that side of our brains all the time. Perhaps we over-think and over-reason our problems to the point where we can't heal on the heart level. (Exit to right-brain here!) Panic is far from logical. If we try to reason it out, we won't get anywhere but highly annoyed! Our intelligence frustrates our battle because we can't make sense of what is happening to us and why.

We're Creative

Fortunately, we don't solely live in our left-brain. That's the good news! We also have well-developed, right-brain, creative sides as well. They may not be as strong as the left, but we still have a large capacity for creativity.

Are you a creative person? Do you enjoy activities involving the imagination? This is the side of your brain that can help you heal the most. If only we could have a flip top head and yank out our left, reasoning side temporarily so we could live in creativity, emotions, and feelings! We might heal quicker (though slightly brain-damaged). Not to worry! I have so many creative outlets that helped me in my journey, and I'll share them all with you in later chapters.

Why Must We Be Perfect?

Am I the only perfectionist in the group? I think not. If we weren't so insistent on being perfect, we'd have less anxiety. Much of my anxiety with dating was thinking, *I'm going to do something to make myself look stupid! Something royally embarrassing! Will my actions send this guy bolting for the nearest exit? Will he walk away?*

I tried to be perfect in so many areas of my life, not just on dates. I knew if I pushed myself hard enough, I'd succeed. For example, in school, I was so driven that I used to set my own assignment schedule that was much faster than the class requirements. I had to be way ahead. Otherwise, I'd feel out of control. (I won't talk about the time I wrote a twenty-paged research paper long before it was due, only to have my professor drop that assignment from our syllabus. Sometimes my drive comes back to bite me.)

Have you noticed we demand perfection of ourselves, yet we hardly expect others to be perfect? We say to ourselves, "I must do everything right." Yet, when someone we know or love messes up, we don't usually greet them with condemnation—not the same condemnation with which we greet ourselves! We realize they're only human. So, why can't we give ourselves that same forgiveness and grace? Why do we place impossible expectations on ourselves, then, feel disappointed when we don't live up to the impossible? Doesn't that sound like setting ourselves up to fail?

I tried to act perfect around guys (in hiding my problems) because I felt no one could love and accept the real, imperfect me. I tried to be a person I thought a guy would want. At my core, I always felt unloved, not chosen, not treasured. I felt I was not worth the trouble for any guy, so I had to be ready to show guys the fake version of me.

How Low Can We Go?

When we feel unloved or unaccepted for who we are, it's no wonder we develop low self-esteems. When we can't live up to our demands for perfection (which, by the way, are impossible to start with), we feel horrible about ourselves. We believe we are failures.

Panic has placed me in such mortifying situations. (Oh, how I'd love to forget!) I felt embarrassed to be the *me* who tried to date. I had better self-esteem in other areas of my life, where my talents and abilities could shine. That's why I spent so much time not dating. If I focused solely on other dreams and goals, I could feel better about myself.

I viewed my worth through the dark glasses of my own low opinion of myself. Then I threw in the low opinion I believed others had of me. However, we cannot look to other people to validate who we are. We can't give them that power over us! We need to take ownership of our identity. We need to know it's okay to be ourselves, who God made us to be. We need to be able to walk into a room and face others without fear, based on who we are in Christ. God's unconditional love validates who we are.

So, why do we feel the need to hide our faults and who we are? We don't have to! Hiding our true selves and our problems takes far too much energy and produces much stress and anxiety.

Our Lord is the only one whose opinion should matter to us. As the Bible says in Jude 24 (kjv), "Now unto him that is able to keep you from falling, and to present you faultless before the presence of his glory with exceeding joy."

Why Must We Be In Control?

The next common trait many of us share is the need for control. We want control of our emotions, feelings, lives, and circumstances. Why must we be in control 100% of the time? No one else around us is. Why do we put that stipulation on ourselves?

Does God ask us to control our lives? Actually, He asks for quite the opposite. As Proverbs 3:5–6 (kjv) says, "Trust in the Lord with all thine heart and lean not unto thine own understanding; in all thy ways acknowledge him, and he shall direct thy paths." Where in that verse does it demand we control our lives and handle our challenges alone?

This verse encourages us not to depend on ourselves but to trust God instead.

For many years, I had amazing control over my emotions. Don't mistake that for bragging. It took me a long time to realize this was not an asset. I used to go six months without crying; it was my claim to fame. If something hurt me, I refused to show it. My persona announced to the world that everything was fine; nothing bothered me.

It wasn't until a few years ago that I finally learned to be human. I let myself feel, let myself admit when something hurt me, and learned how to admit faults and vulnerabilities. Talk about the most freeing character change I ever went through!

It all started when I finally decided to tell people about my anxiety problem.

My panic problem was the one area where I had no control. As you can tell from parts of my story I've shared so far, I had ways of trying to hide it, trying to control it—publicly. In general, panic is a loss of control.

Depression Runs Rampant

Isn't it hard not to add depression on top of self-loathing or lack of acceptance? Not everyone who has an anxiety disorder is depressed, but many times they go together. Depression is a problem that brings its own set of characteristics outside what you're already experiencing with anxiety. It's common for us to go through both. I know I did! I became depressed when panic seemed to be ruining my life and any hopes I'd live through a relationship.

We Share Common Fears

The last commonality is that we tend to fear the same fears. When you pinpoint what you are afraid of, most likely it will fall under one of these categories:

Fear of abandonment
Fear of rejection
Fear of the opinions of others
Fear of pain (physically or emotionally)
Fear of risk
Fear of loss
Fear of death

Many of my experiences taught me that these fears were valid. For example, I had several relationships where men walked away early on, during the height of my anxiety struggles. I had few relationships that lasted more than a month. I felt like people were always leaving me.

My next conclusion—though erroneous—seemed logical: *my fears of abandonment are valid because people always walk away once they get to know me.* I fed myself the message that I should fear relationships because of the risk of that person leaving. Therefore, my panic disorder then served as my defense mechanism. In truth, I was pushing these men away, rejecting them before they could reject me. The guys may have been the ones to say "it's time to break up", but I kept them at arm's length to keep them from hurting me. This made having healthy relationships virtually impossible.

So, while it may have looked like them running for the nearest exit confirmed my fears, it was my fears that drove them away. The cycle was set up—I could not win—not until I learned to face my disorder.

Cheryl's Journal (1996)
It's hard to trust that anyone will be interested in staying in a relationship because so far no one has. It's a pattern thing, I guess, that makes me think no one ever will.

I believed this lie for such a long time. I never trusted anyone to stay, to care enough about me that they could help me past the stages of the relationship where panic was rampant. Panic became my defense mechanism; it became my way of keeping guys away from me. It was the only way I could ensure I wouldn't get hurt. Yet, I was hurting anyway! I failed to see that my so-called protector was my enemy.

One time in my journal, I wrote about the wall I put between guys and me:

> *Cheryl's Journal (February 1996)*
> *I have boundary problems. I probably put up too many. The good side is I'm not giving into what I shouldn't, like sex before I'm married. But I also don't tell all. Instead, I tell nothing. I put up too many walls. This way, I never let anyone get close.*

Malcolm Smith in *Freedom from Fear* says, "Probably the greatest fear is in the realm of our being loved. We are constantly anxious that we will not measure up to other people's standards and will be rejected by them. Our nightmare is to go through life unloved and unwanted by anyone." (2)

When we put ourselves out where we could be rejected, we risk getting hurt. Sometimes we avoid situations where we could be rejected to protect ourselves. Is this where you want to stay — protected, yet, not living? I lived there for so long. I had to choose to get out of the boat — even riding tsunamis — in order to restore my life.

You can, too, if you're willing to take the risk. As I've mentioned, I watched many of my dreams die because my fears ran out of control. Do you have any dreams you'd like to revive — dreams you could possibly reach if you decided to take the risk?

Let's stop here to reflect on what some of those dreams are.

ASSIGNMENT:

Take out your journal to write down what your dreams are for your life. What would you like to accomplish? Are your fears stopping you? If so, which

fears? Has your anxiety disorder gotten in the way? Make a list of goals you would try to reach if you had no fears about the consequences of trying. Make a list of what you feel you have to lose. Then make a list of what you feel you have to gain.

I hope, by the time you're done with this book, you'll feel the irresistible drive to go after any dreams you've left behind. Hopefully, that drive will be stronger than the drive to protect yourself from risk and pain.

Life At Home

In the next chapter, I will tell you about the relationship that drove me to reach out and get help, to finally go for counseling. Before I get to that, I would like to share a bit about my family life and how I grew up.

I became a Christian at a young age. God was always an important part of my family's life. I was raised by my amazing parents—they're like each other's best friend. They clearly loved each other, and they loved my older sister, Heather, and me. Heather loved me almost as much as she loved torturing me.

I grew up in Massachusetts. When I was eleven, my parents decided to move us to North Carolina. The school we attended up north was getting rough and so were some of the friends I made. My parents wanted my sister and me to go to a Christian school in North Carolina. It was a sacrifice on their part—their business was in Massachusetts—but they strongly believed Heather and I needed to be in a better school.

So we moved.

We moved to North Carolina in 1983, just one year before my first anxiety attack. I was in sixth grade. While I missed my family and friends in Massachusetts, I was excited to move to a new place and make new friends. Some of the best friends I still have in my life today are friends I met that year at my new school.

From a young age, my parents were great about teaching me how to set goals and chase dreams. They taught me I could be whatever I wanted to be, achieve any dream I set my heart and mind to. It's one of the benefits I appreciate most about my upbringing. They were always positive and upbeat, encouraging me no matter what dreams I chased after. They even supported me when I wanted to be an actress destined for Hollywood. (What parent wants to hear that?)

Once my sister and I were teenagers, my parents continued to travel back and forth to Massachusetts to keep their business going. My parents put a lot of trust in us, leaving us at home. I credit them with my independence and sense of responsibility. Everyone always thought I was older than I was. I took responsibility to the extreme and acted as though I were my older sister's mother. (She never appreciated that. Wonder why!) I wanted to be a trustworthy kid because my parents believed in me.

Unfortunately, I chose to hide my imperfections from my parents. This included my anxiety problems. I wanted them to believe I could take care of myself; I didn't want them to see my weaknesses. This was a conscious choice I made, not something they ever expected from me. I wanted to be an adult and self-sufficient long before my time. They never demanded perfection. Even if Heather and I did mess up, it's not like the consequences were horrible. I was grounded once my entire teen life; for one excruciating week, I couldn't use the telephone. (What a tragic week during my adolescent existence!)

During these teen years, I hid my emotions. I never wanted anyone to see me cry, so I kept myself in control. Thankfully, I worked out my emotions on paper (which is why so many journal entries exist). Writing was my only outlet, my own version of self-therapy, and I didn't even know it.

I developed all of these defenses that put on a face that said *everything's fine* when inside I was dying. I felt trapped in a body I couldn't stand because it was so imperfect; I couldn't control it from panicking. The amount of time I spent pretending was ridiculous. If I had just been honest and asked for help, this darkness would never have gone on as long as it did. My outward persona may have sent the message that I was in perfect condition; but inside, I was far from healthy. The irony is, I was a terrific actress in real life, putting on this persona. Yet as you know, when I tried to make it as a theatrical actress, teachers and directors told me I was far too inhibited with my emotions.

I worked hard to hide *potential* ups and downs in my life as well. For example, I didn't talk much about auditions, for fear of having to say I didn't get the part. I never used to tell anyone if I had a date. That way, if I got stood up, I was the only one who would know. I didn't want anyone to know if I got rejected for anything. I wanted to weather those disappointments alone.

Sometimes, I would keep it a secret from my parents when I was dating someone. I knew the inevitable breakup would come. If they didn't know I was dating, they wouldn't have to find out I'd gone through a breakup either. (I always knew the breakup would come quickly after dating began. I was used to that pattern!) I didn't want them to know I felt pain.

For anyone to know I had feelings or had been through a painful experience felt embarrassing. I wanted everyone to believe I was strong—fearless—when I was anything but fearless. I was going out with Greg for six weeks before my father took a phone message from him and asked who he was. I didn't explain much at all, didn't say he was a very important boyfriend in my life, didn't say he was the reason I ended up in the hospital just a few weeks earlier.

I know it's not logical, but it's the way I lived. That's why panic was such an enemy! It worked against everything I stood for: control, perfection, fearlessness. That's why panic entered my life; I wasn't letting my emotions come out in normal ways. Our bodies will take on physical reactions to emotions we refuse to let ourselves feel. Just think of how many people get stomach ulcers from stress.

I may have sailed alone, but I didn't have to. I didn't have to be so secretive with my family. I didn't have to run away from dating, but I did, for a long time. When I decided to try again—in December of 1995—the panics started all over again. This time, they were the worst I'd ever experienced. I had to face that I had not gotten better; my avoidance hadn't cured me.

And neither had God.

CHAPTER 4
Valleys:
When God Doesn't Heal...
Right Away

The wise man in the storm prays to God, not for safety
from danger, but for deliverance from fear.
(Ralph Waldo Emerson)

Have you ever wondered why God lets us suffer?

Thankfully, God knows how to turn bad situations around for His glory. I believe we go through challenges in our lives for a reason. It may be years before we understand the good that can come from suffering. God has our big picture in His hands. He knows the whys, the hows, the whens. We are not privy to that information. However, because we trust God, we have to know He has our best interests at heart. So, what do we do while we endure the pain, the trials?

There are many ministries that promote prayer for miraculous healing. They imply that if you just pray right — then believe — you will be healed. While I believe this works for some people and for some conditions, I also firmly believe there are times when a surface healing or an immediate healing may not be in our best interests.

I begged God — over and over — to heal me, but was that in my best interest? Was just taking away my anxiety disorder the right action for God to take? I didn't even know why I had it! Clearly, I had some healing to do that would not have been accomplished if God just took my symptoms away. I wished with all my heart that He would have, but I didn't understand what I was asking for.

God knew better when He chose not answer my prayers in the way I asked. I spent years angry with God because He hadn't healed me. God and I had work to do; I had to stop fighting Him before I could even start down the road to healing. I had seeds I needed to sow before I could reap the harvest of healing. Most importantly, God wanted my surrender and trust.

To follow is a rough journal entry. This is some of the darkest stuff I'd written, during a season of despair. I share it because I want to give you a peek into how bad it got, how alone and forgotten I felt by God:

Cheryl's Journal

What exactly does one do with a broken life? How does one pick up the pieces of a shattered existence? When rationality doesn't work, when the brain just leaps to illogical thought, what does one do to get out of it? How does one not give in to a life of making bad choices out of pain? How does one keep her sanity? How does one quiet the voices of darkness when the Voice of Light isn't saying anything?

We're supposed to have hope, yet our expectations are always wrong. We get disappointed. Is it better to have no hope? Which way is the right way to live? We can't expect anything to happen that we want to happen. Yet if we hope, we're doing exactly that. What is it like to live void of hopes and dreams? I think I'm about to find out.

I feel dead. Pointless. I'd like to at least shut my emotions off so I don't have to feel the depravity. Numb them. My mind isn't functioning from the place I'm used to living. I'm lifeless and joyless, and God has done nothing to correct this situation. It's so hard for me not to be angry.

Where is God with the solution? I thought He would at least be there to heal me from all the pain. Instead, He must be just watching me wander around aimlessly, void of any sense of life, hope, love, creativity. I can't even write. Might as well strip me of everything. Why not? I've done things "right" my whole life and I see where it's gotten me. Completely suicidal and hopeless.

This isn't me talking. I am letting other forces in, I guess. I don't know why God isn't stronger than them. I don't want them. I've asked God to help me over and over. It's not like I've been ignoring God. If He meets us where we are, where is He when I need Him?

If I were being rational these words would sound beyond ridiculous. I don't feel accountable to these words right now because I don't feel like me. I am lost and sinking deeper.

Those words are typical of many journal entries. I had to work out so much of my pain on paper because I had no idea what else to do with my pain.

It was during my next serious relationship that my anger with God for not offering an instant healing intensified.

A Secret Crush

I had refused to date for so many years.

Then, in walks a man I'll call Nathan. I met Nathan in grad school in 1993. He was a mysterious, interesting man with a deep faith in God. I knew quite a few women in grad school who were drawn to him. There was just something about him: something intimidating, yet exciting. Nathan was almost six years older than I was, a PhD student, and the producer of several scripts I wrote. (He loved telling me what to do!)

I started developing feelings for him. Never in a million years did I think he'd ever return those feelings, so liking him was in some ways safe. This was around the time I had just learned the name of my panic disorder, through the Michael English interviews. I knew what my problem was, but I didn't know why I had it. Because Nathan and I were just friends, I wasn't struggling too much with my nerves.

This was the only season of my life I didn't look forward to weekends. They meant I wouldn't have a chance to run into Nathan; I only saw him on class days. During the week, I scoped out the parking lot at school to see if his car were there. (I still remember his license plate number!) My stomach would leap if I spotted his car. I'd walk the halls where he had an office, hoping to run into him — purely by accident, of course. And, yes, he made me nervous. But in this case — unlike with Kirk — hiding this crush kept my anxiety manageable.

I did, however, trick Nathan into taking me on a fake date. He lost a bet with two other girlfriends of mine and me. Our prize: he was to take all three of us out. My conniving self purposely set the schedule for his chance to pay up on a night neither of the other women could go. That was bold for me! I was nervous. It wasn't a real date, but I had a tough time making it through dinner. That night, I didn't have an attack, but I knew my anxiety problem wasn't gone.

During the summer of 1994, Nathan and I fostered a strong friendship. We started hanging out a lot, outside of class projects. (Weekends became fun again!) The friendship lines started to blur. We'd hang out late, sometimes until four in the morning, either at his place or at the beach. We'd talk about our lives, our histories, and most importantly, God. We'd wrestle with issues about our faith. He was such an encouragement to me in my walk with the Lord. He was the deepest person I'd ever communicated with. I didn't need much sleep when I hung around him; he brought a new energy into my life. I loved having a crush on him. It had been such a long time since I'd felt anything for a guy! He appeared interested in me, yet he wasn't acting on it.

That summer, Nathan left town for a week (during which time he let me borrow the car with the aforementioned, memorized license plate number). I earnestly sought God about Nathan while he was away.

I felt like God's answer to me was "not now."

I knew when Nathan got back into town our relationship would have to change. I had to stop putting myself in situations with him that stirred up my feelings, the times that made me wonder if there were more to our friendship.

However, when Nathan returned, he also seemed different. I didn't have to address anything because our friendship normalized. I assumed nothing would ever grow beyond friendship, even though God's answer, "not now," was open-ended.

The Turning Point

When I graduated in the summer of 1995, I moved back to North Carolina where my family lived. Nathan was still in school. We visited each other often, still just as friends. In fact, during one of my visits I went up to see a different guy I had a spontaneous, mini-fling with. That was such a fluke! So unlike me. The anxiety I experienced over that was when I knew it shouldn't continue. In fact, I was talking about it with Nathan when I almost had a panic attack at 6 a.m. over breakfast. Nathan asked, "What is wrong with you? I've never seen you so unfocused." I tried to act normally and did not explain what was happening as I shoved what was probably a yummy IHOP waffle aside.

In December 1995, a year and a half after our summer of the *undefined* friendship, everything changed. I'll never forget the night at my house when Nathan and I decided we'd stay up all night and play cards. He had to be at the airport early to head to his parents' home for Christmas. So instead of me heading off to my room, him heading off to the guestroom, we thought we'd play gin rummy.

While playing, he slipped in a comment about how, during the summer of 1994, our relationship was unclear. I almost fell off my chair; I couldn't believe he was acknowledging that season in our friendship! We'd never talked about it. My hands started to sweat, my stomach churned a bit. I didn't respond to his comment, didn't even look at him. The jack of spades appeared far more interesting to me at that moment. Nathan was testing me, to see how I'd react, but I couldn't; I knew I wouldn't make it through the conversation without having a panic attack if I tried. Part of me was excited he mentioned it because it felt like our relationship could go somewhere—a place I'd been wishing for, for over two years!

Nathan left that morning for his parents' place, but he flew back to my town a week later, on his way back to grad school. That is when he finally spoke up about wanting to start a romantic relationship. That had been my dream for so long; I couldn't believe it was happening. It was so rare that someone I had feelings for noticed me, let alone spoke up and asked to be more than friends.

And that's when they started—the worst panic attacks I'd ever had in my life.

The night Nathan asked me to start dating we were at a restaurant, having just finished dinner. (Yes, it was bad timing, but how was he supposed to know that?) I immediately had to leave the table; I got sick in the bathroom. When I came out, I asked if we could go somewhere more private.

I was still hoping to hide my problem, but the symptoms were overpowering me. When we arrived at my car, I waited until he got in first so I could quickly throw up in the parking lot without him seeing. Then I got in the car, trying to act like everything was fine. I wanted to hide it, just like I always had before; I was failing.

When we got to the place where Nathan was staying, I decided that, for the first time, I would tell a guy about my problem—my mysterious problem. We had been such good friends for years. I thought if I didn't try to hide it, it would help undercut some of the symptoms.

Unfortunately, that did not work.

I think I needed a lot of help by that point from a trained counselor; just admitting it wasn't enough. Nathan tried to show his understanding, even though neither one of us understood why this was happening to me. My symptoms didn't stop; I had the worst anxiety attacks I'd ever had. It was horrifying; I was beyond humiliated, frustrated, and angry with God.

I finally had what I'd hoped for — a relationship with this friend right in front of me — and I was messing it up because I couldn't "be normal." (That was my favorite insult to sling at myself. Do you have some of those?)

Why couldn't I just relax? He'd been my amazing friend for over two years! I could trust him, right? Why did dating him bring such a change over me? What was wrong with me?

Even though I'd been willing to admit I had a problem, I still didn't want to show it or have panic attacks every time I saw him. I wanted the problem to go away so we could try to have a successful relationship. I wanted so badly to act *normally*, but I usually failed. The attacks were more intense than when I was younger. I begged God to heal me; He didn't.

In an anxious moment, I did what I do best: I sorted my thoughts out on paper:

Cheryl's Journal (December 31, 1995)

I'm afraid I'm making myself look like an idiot. I'm afraid I'm going to scare him off. This is something I've prayed about for a long time — that this problem would go away. I thought it was gone because I hadn't had any anxiety attacks in five years. Of course, I haven't dated in five years, either. I just assumed the problem was gone. Boy, was I wrong! Maybe this is the thorn in my side that God refuses to take away. I hate this, but maybe it's worth it to deal with this now so I can be with him. I'm afraid that it's going to last longer this time than usual, that I'll never get the chance to get used to him since he doesn't live near me. I hope he can bear with me now that he's seeing me at my worst. Maybe I'm too afraid of the risks involved. This problem is ruining my life.

A few weeks into the relationship, I journaled this:

Cheryl's Journal (January 19, 1996)
   I have anxiety about seeing him. I have no idea how I'm going to get rid of it. It's a lot of pressure to feel like I have to be normal when we only get two days together for each visit. What if I can't control my anxiety? Lessening anxiety feels impossible. Did God bring us together so I could be totally humiliated? Because, so far, that's all I've gotten out of this!

Death of a Longtime Dream

Our relationship lasted a mere six weeks. I couldn't be around Nathan without having attacks. There were those rare moments when I'd get a reprieve, when I'd suddenly be calm for a slice of time throughout the day. But most of the time, I was full of anxiety. It made for such a challenging relationship.

Because we were long-distance, I never had the chance to get used to him in this new way. I was unable to speak my mind about anything; I couldn't communicate about what was going on inside. I closed up. Nathan felt it wasn't working and wanted us to transition back to the friends we had always been.

Because—from my point of view—Nathan wanted to give up so quickly, I fed myself the lie that no guy would stick around long enough for me to get used to him and be calm. I didn't think anyone would ever love me enough to think I was worth the trouble anxiety brought into the relationship. I believed if I were given enough time to get used to a relationship and build a trust, I could at some point calm down. But since most of my relationships ended so quickly, I never got the chance to test that theory. I believed no one would ever choose to stay, treasure me enough, love me enough to see me through this fear.

Did I mention we broke up right around Valentines Day? Yeah, that happened to me again. I despised that commercialized holiday!

While Nathan wanted to go right back to being friends, for me, it wasn't so easy. I desperately wanted to stay friends because he was so important to me, but my anxiety attacks wouldn't stop. I still couldn't be near him, even as much as six months after we stopped dating.

Cheryl's Journal (July 5, 1996)

These past few days have been incredibly draining emotionally and physically. I feel like I'm at the lowest I've ever been with this problem. I'm not usually an overly emotional person, but I'm disappointed that I'm not getting any better. I do all this work — the anxiety tapes, the relaxation methods. I'm nowhere. I am just as bad as when I started. I can't think or move. I keep phasing out. I feel like I'm going crazy. I can feel the tenseness in my neck, my jaw, my arms, my stomach. My exercises don't help. Thought-stopping seems impossible. And how do I just ignore symptoms like books suggest? I'd dearly like to know. They're just there, screaming for attention. I feel like I'm adding depression to my list of problems. I cry out to God, but I can't tell He's there even though I beg for some encouragement. Why does He always seem so far away? Why is He gone for my lowest points? I know in my head He's not but how do I convince my heart? I watch myself acting like this and want to just snap out of it. I want to be normal again. I sit staring out this window, asking God why, begging for any relief. It doesn't come. This is something I've grown to hate, despise, dread, fear. There aren't enough words to say it. The debilitating attacks of anxiety that leave me feeling alone, forsaken.

I was distressed. I don't believe all that I wrote, but I was being honest about how I felt. There's much to be said about coping techniques—even the ones I felt had failed me—and about God and His role in my recovery. But I just wanted to share with you honestly some of the thoughts I had contemplated during my low points. That night, I was in bed for sleepless hours, crying, trying to push my own skin off. I hated being in my skin, but it wouldn't move. It stayed there, and I lie helpless, uncomfortable, wishing my bed would just swallow me whole. I—in a removed way—knew that what I was doing was insane, but at the same time, I couldn't stop myself. I felt too uncomfortable being myself.

It took me eight months to be able to be around Nathan without having anxiety attacks. (Today, we are still friends.) I'm thankful we took the chance because one of the most important parts of my healing came out of that relationship—it drove me to seek counseling. I will talk about that experience in the next chapter.

Which Way Did God Go?

You may be asking, like I was: where was God in all of this? While God was a huge part of my recovery, I don't want to ignore the big question: Why doesn't God heal right away? Why does He let us suffer?

My friend, Christa Sands, author of *Learning to Trust Again*, voiced this struggle in her book: "Pain is God's warning signal that something needs to be brought to the Healer. [God] wants to help us face the truth. He wants to carry us through it all. God desires wholeness for us, yet He cannot heal the parts of ourselves that we deny exist. Letting go of our protection may seem impossible, but it is fundamental to healing.... Growth doesn't happen unless we face our fears.... God does have the power to heal instantly, but I believe He most often works His miracle of emotional healing over time. Our character is defined as we persevere through pain. It was very difficult, but I had to learn to be patient in order to see God heal the deepest parts of me." (1)

In moments of dark despair I felt such a loss of control; I hated myself and my ugly weakness. I thought the Lord, known as the Prince of Peace, had left me during the darkest moments of my life.

I couldn't see Him with the eyes of my heart. I hated being on the wrong side of faith—down that road called mistrust. I had to discover with my heart that when He said He'd never leave me, He meant it. But that was no easy road to find!

God's Stoplight

Don't beat yourself up if you experience anger toward God, especially when He closes a door on something you've prayed about for so long. King David used to cry out through the Psalms all the time, sometimes saying he felt like God had left him. He eventually realized God was still there. Yet there were those times David felt abandoned, and he was willing to be honest about that and tell God how he felt. So can we. I think God would rather have us go to Him with honesty, with our pain, than hide our feelings. He sees right through us anyway, right?

God is sovereign and chooses to do things His way. We can get in the way of His ways, override His will. When He chooses not to honor our requests the way we want Him to, it only proves His faithfulness to us. He is all-knowing; He knows above all else what is best for us. When He doesn't answer our prayers the way we ask Him to, He has something different or better in mind.

For a long time, I didn't understand why He said no to me when I begged for healing. I came to realize that if God had just offered me some miracle cure and had taken the anxiety away without me doing any work, I would have fallen back into my old habits and ways of thinking quickly. That would have gotten me nowhere.

Think of a man who gets lung cancer. Let's say God heals him. If that man returns to smoking, it would be easy for cancer to invade his body again. Emotional problems are no different. God's instant healing will not do us any good if we have no idea what got us into that state. Panic rarely comes out of nowhere, even if it feels like it does.

In hindsight, I realize a miracle cure would not have been best for me. After much searching, I felt like God told me there were certain things in my life, certain beliefs I held, bitterness from the past I had never let go of. I had to deal with those before I would ever be ready to handle a relationship in a healthy way.

Once I quit trying to get God to heal me and started asking Him what I needed to do, what I needed to face, whom I needed to forgive, my progress began. God helped me become a whole person for the first time in my life.

ASSIGNMENT:

The Bible clearly states, "For God hath not given us the spirit of fear; but of power, and of love, and of a sound mind" (2 Timothy 1:7 kjv). Fear does not come from God. Reflect on the following question: What would your actions be if you were released from your panic disorder? Is it possible the release from fear would lead you down a path toward sin? This will not apply to all panic situations, and God does not send us fear to keep us from sinning. Just take a closer look at your life to figure out if a release from this fear will expose an area of weakness to sin that could drive you further away from God. If it's possible that it will, God may withhold the answer to your prayers for your own good and for your own protection until you have allowed Him to strengthen you enough in that area.

During this time of struggles when you may be questioning God's faithfulness, I have an exercise that can build your faith.

ASSIGNMENT:

Go back over your life and reflect on the times

when God has been faithful. There's no way to remember them all, but jot down what you do remember in a list, a list you can access whenever you feel you are losing faith. Write down times He's helped you get through something, supplied something you needed, or even just gave you a gift you wanted. The list can grow over time. Keep a record and add to it often.

God's Road Toward Trials

Did God promise us that our lives would be perfect when we chose to follow Him? No. Actually, He tried to prepare us that sometimes, it would feel like the opposite. He promised trials, problems, and hard times, but He also promised never to leave us or forsake us (Hebrews 13:5).

I think God does us a favor in these cases. He doesn't just wipe the pain away, especially a pain we never took the time to admit and feel. We have to live through it, not deny it. We need to take the time to be victims, if necessary, before we can move on.

Are you angry with God for your trials? I'll share something that helped me with my anger. I realized that every time I said I was angry, it was always with God and never with Jesus. I wondered, *Why am I always mad at God and not Jesus? How can I be mad at Jesus? He came down here to save me, died on the cross for my sins. I can't be mad at Him.* And then it dawned on me! God is the loving Father who sent that Son to die for me. If I can't be mad at Jesus, I shouldn't be mad at God. It put things in perspective for me. So, next time you're angry with God, tell Jesus about it and see if that helps deflate your anger.

I will continue to share God's important role in my recovery. He proved over and over that He has never left me—and He never will. In fact, He's carried me. I've had to accept that God is still my God, even when He doesn't heal right away or in the ways that I ask.

If you find that you are not progressing through prayers for healing, that is not God's fault. It's also not your fault! Don't heap guilt on yourself like I did, believing you must not have prayed right or had the right faith. It just means you have more work to do.

As Dr. Hart says, "Anxiety is disruptive enough without adding the shame and guilt of feeling rejected by God. Feelings of guilt and worthlessness abound among Christian believers who suffer from anxiety because they incorrectly assume that their problem is a sign of personal failure or of God's disapproval.... Times of anxiety are not necessarily times when we have no faith.... I have no doubt that God *can* miraculously restore your self-confidence—but He may not choose to do it... Who knows why He does not always heal? We must trust God's great wisdom in this matter and begin to work on the problem ourselves, depending on Him for the strength and courage we need to face our fears." (2)

Psalm 34:14 (kjv) says, "Depart from evil, and do good; seek peace, and pursue it." Pursuing peace means going after it, working toward it, planting seeds of peace but having to wait for the fruit of it to come forth. We have to sow before we can reap, plant before we can harvest. This, by nature, implies time will be necessary before we can see the fruit of our labor.

Healing Words

In the first chapter, I mentioned how important it is to learn to listen for God's voice to heal. I'd like to end this chapter with some beautiful words I feel God said to me when I was praying about the issue of walking through trials. However, I do want to state clearly that we can make mistakes in our journaling as we listen for God's voice.

I will share throughout this book what I believe God has told me, in hopes that it can be an encouragement to you as well. Just understand that I am also human, and I can make mistakes. (Yes, I'm admitting I am not perfect.)

I believe God spoke to me, met me where I was, and poured out His healing words straight into my heart. This journal session was written eight years after counseling. I feel it applies here because it explains why God may withhold a healing for a season, for our own good. To follow is my conversation with God:

Cheryl's Journal (2004)

Cheryl's prayer: "Lord, why does life have to be so painful? So full of trials?"

God's reply: "Pour out your complaints to Me. Empty your soul. I can handle the burden. I was made to carry your burdens and your grievances. I know you feel anger, and that's okay. Give it to Me. Let Me turn it into something usable. You are not alone and you will never be alone. I am with you, beside you. I see your heart. Stay in tune and in communion with Me. I know you're hurting. Let Me walk with you. I'll walk you to your next destination. I'll stay with you. It's hard for you to be thankful when you're enduring pain. It's hard to see the good and especially the good you are turning into by enduring trials. There are changes that take place below the surface, changes you don't even see. But I see them! It's beautiful. And My hand is at work inside you. It may be painful at times, but it's necessary. I see your larger picture, the one you can't see. It's there. If you could see down the road, you'd rejoice greatly, loudly. I see down that road. You can't; yet I want you to rejoice anyway. Understand that it's all in My hands. Have that faith. Know that I am capable. I am at the end of that line and at each step between. I don't minimize your pain. I help you endure it."

Cheryl's prayer: "When does life become what I want it to be?"

God's reply: "Your life is not your own, Cheryl. You gave it to Me to use as I please. And yes, that means you endure trials. But you never walk through them alone and without purpose. I am the One who heals and restores.

*Remember, I am sovereign. Trust in Me. What doesn't make sense now one day will. I never promised I'd make sense. I promised to love you, to save you, to endure fires with you. And that is enough. Accept that blessing. I will not put you in a situation that is more than you can handle. I care about your heart. You can stop being suspect of that. I treasure you and your love. I take care of you in all circumstances. I see the holes you think you have. I want to fill those. I don't want you looking to everything else to fill those holes. Look to Me. Make Me enough. Everything else will follow. You are still My child when you cry. You are still My child when you yell and scream and even throw a tantrum. You are My child no matter how you feel or act. You are Mine. There is a way for you to experience joy despite circumstances. It's through having faith in Me, trusting in Me, and understanding that My timing is perfect and right. As you surrender to Me and don't work against Me, I can move and work. You are in tune with Me and that's what I ask for and need from you. I am the Rewarder of those who seek Me. Seek Me with all your heart, mind, and soul. I see your heart. I know every ounce of it and the pain that runs through it. Entrust it to Me, as I restore you. I am the Restorer. Don't question My heart and My motives. Your good is always first and foremost on My heart. That is secure. **Rest in the power of My love that is far-reaching beyond any love you can find on this earth.**"*

Isn't that beautiful? God's words spoken to my heart were more soothing than any medicine I could have taken.

If you haven't already, I hope you'll learn to discern His still, small voice. I never would have healed without it. God was the only One who could penetrate the walls around my heart and offer me a chance to heal, a chance to live the life I was meant to live, a chance to chase all the dreams I had left behind, a chance to become whole.

Your journey toward healing can start now. Continue down the path with God, as the rest of this book is the journey toward healing and peace.

PART II
The Journey

CHAPTER 5
Reading the Signs:
Guided Through Therapy

Cheryl's Journal (February 1996)

Lord, my relationship with Nathan is now over. I don't understand it, but I realize this has been a time of personal growth. Even if the only purpose dating him served was to point out I need help, that's worth the pain. Lord, my prayer is that you bring someone into my life, like a counselor, who can help me deal with these issues. Obviously, I can't try to have any more relationships until I get help. It's sad, but obviously for now it's best. I think I need to be a whole person; I have some rebuilding to do. Well, maybe we have some rebuilding to do — You and me. I doubt I can do this on my own.

I was twelve years old when I had my first anxiety attack. I was twenty-four when I stepped into my first counseling session. Why did it take me so long to get there? Pride. Denial. Confusion. Fear.

Once I admitted my problem to my private self, I thought, *I can't admit this to someone else. Especially not someone I don't know.* For some people, admitting challenges to a counselor — rather than a friend or family member — is easier. I didn't want to admit my problems to anyone, stranger or not. I also had a hang-up when it came to the idea of therapy. *That's for sick people,* I protested. Then I admitted I needed healing from something. I finally decided it was worth asking for help.

Do you go to the doctor when there is something physically wrong? If you don't take care of your mental health, you can end up with physical problems, too. Since anxiety is riddled with physical symptoms, it's important to take care of the problem as soon as possible or it can damage your body.

A Time For Action

After my relationship with Nathan ended, I decided it was time to admit it: I had a problem. I was never going to have love in my life if I didn't do something about it. I decided twelve years was enough of trying to fix it on my own. I wasn't doing a good job, anyway. I didn't want the rest of my life to be void of relationships because I couldn't control my panic attacks. I had always wanted a husband and a family. How was I supposed to reach that goal if I couldn't get within inches of a guy I liked and not have an attack?

So, my walk through therapy began. It started with the Yellow Pages. I had no desire at all to tell anyone about my thoughts on getting help; therefore, I couldn't ask for referrals. When I looked in the Yellow Pages, I felt drawn to a Christian counseling ministry. When I called, I didn't tell the guy on the other end of the line anything except that I had little money and wanted only to talk to a woman. He immediately asked, "Is the nature of your problem with relationships and anxiety?" *How did he know?* I wondered. I immediately felt God's confirmation and peace that this was the right place.

I stepped into that counseling office, my knees a bit shaky. I decided it was normal to be nervous about a first-time counseling session. Thankfully, I didn't have an attack.

The most helpful device I got from therapy was the journal exercises my counselor gave me to do between sessions. I share many of them in this book because they are questions I had to answer to get better. I did at least two hours worth of work on journal questions per week: poking, prodding, probing, remembering, reflecting, crying, laughing. My therapist felt my willingness to work would be key to my healing.

I wrote the following after my first counseling session:

> *Cheryl's Journal (March 1996)*
>
> *My counselor suggests getting sick is my defense, my way of protecting myself from feeling, hiding from my emotions. It keeps people away from me and me away from them. That makes sense. I'm so out of touch with my feelings. I have the feeling before this is over, I'll have to open up in more ways than I want to and to more people than I want to. But if it means improving, I will.*

I encourage you to take an active part in your own recovery as well. Don't depend solely on those fifty-minute sessions per week. It's up to you to do the work, not the therapist. Like I told my counselor, I didn't want to stay in therapy. The only way to get out was to do the work.

Try not to breeze over the assignments in this book. They are important. Just reading the questions won't help. Take time to answer them — in writing and in detail. I am going to share with you some of the many questions I answered during my months in therapy.

Exploration Through Questions

Answer as many of the following questions as possible in your *Finally Fearless Workbook* or journal. Skip the ones that don't apply to your situation. Take your time. Don't feel you have to answer them all before you continue reading this book. The answers should not be rushed.

ANXIETY QUESTIONS:

Describe situations when you have experienced full-blown anxiety attacks. Be detailed.

In what situations can you predict that anxiety will happen?

Is there anything you are doing that is feeding this problem?

Does panic keep you away from anything? Stop you from experiencing anything?

Is there a sinful side of anxiety? Consider what the Bible says about being anxious. Do you feel guilty for having anxiety? Is it a sign of a lack of faith? Is it a sin?

If fighting an attack makes it worse, what can you replace fighting with? What can you do instead? What will make you feel like you're being productive during an attack to stop it, without making it worse?

Do you need to know why you have an anxiety disorder? If so, why is it important that you pinpoint the cause?

What causes you to feel anxiety? (Ex. insecurity, fear of rejection)

How do you talk to and relate to people? How do you handle yourself socially? Does being social bring on anxiety?

Are there any friends who make you feel more comfortable during an anxiety attack? If so, describe what they do to help the situation. Pinpoint qualities in them that make you feel calmer. When they are around, do they bring out different qualities in you? Do you lose inhibitions?

Given your particular situation, describe how you'd be in that situation if you didn't panic. What would change?

What feelings does panic bring out of you?

What purpose does panic serve?

Personify your fear: What does it look like to you? Describe it as though it were a person in your life.

REJECTION QUESTIONS:

When in your life have you felt rejected? Did you know at the time it was a rejection? Was it really a rejection?

How do you deal with rejection? What mechanisms do you have to handle rejection?

What's the worst that can happen to you when you're rejected?

Evaluate exactly what is rejected: You as a person? A personality trait? An idea or belief that you hold? Is it likely the rejection has nothing to do with you personally? If it is you, does that mean something has to change? Are these changes for your own good? Or, if changes occur, are they only to please the person who did the rejecting?

What makes you feel intimidated by a person?

EMBARRASSMENT QUESTIONS:

When have you been humiliated?

What embarrasses you?

When have you been embarrassed because of your emotions? Were you just embarrassed to show them or were you embarrassed to feel them?

When have you hidden your emotions so you wouldn't be embarrassed?

Why do you hide truths about your life, like disappointments?

Do you fight tears when you need to cry? Do you only let yourself cry if you feel other people will think the situation warrants that reaction?

Are there situations where anyone reacted poorly to your emotions? Your tears? Has anyone ever told you that you shouldn't feel the way you're feeling, and therefore, invalidated your feelings?

UPBRINGING / FAMILY LIFE QUESTIONS:
Take a closer look at why you hide your troubles from friends or family. Do you have any past examples when you did tell them something that was hard to tell?

What would happen if you did share something that was bothering you emotionally?

What would happen if you shared an imperfection? A fault?

What role did image and appearances play in your upbringing?

MISCELLANEOUS QUESTIONS:
Do people's opinions of you affect what you think of yourself and your abilities (professionally and personally)?

In what areas are you afraid of taking risks?

How do you handle conflicts? Confrontations? Do you speak up when someone makes you angry? Can you clearly speak about your feelings?

How do you feel about change and uncertainty?

How do you handle loss? The fear of loss?

What does fear look like?

Why do you always have to be in control?

Why do you feel like you are not worth the effort for people? Why do you feel unlovable?

Who accepts you unconditionally? What do they do to make you feel accepted? Is there anyone who does not accept you unconditionally?

When have you not gotten the attention you craved?

When have you not gotten the attention you needed?

What kinds of barriers do you have up? Why do you think they are there? What can you do to knock them down? Can you ask others to do anything to help you knock them down?

My Voyage Through Answers

To follow are several examples of my answers to some of those questions:

QUESTION: IN WHAT SITUATIONS CAN YOU PREDICT THAT ANXIETY WILL HAPPEN?

"I can always predict when I'll start having anxiety attacks. It's at the beginning of every relationship. Every time when I will see the person, especially soon before they come to pick me up. The hour before is usually the worst. Once I see them, I sometimes calm down, but not always. I was usually uneasy in relationships for at least the first month—mainly, only when I'd see them. However, additional times with one particular relationship, I would even get sick if we were talking on the phone. At least that was easier to hide from the guy."

QUESTION: HOW DO YOU TALK TO AND RELATE TO PEOPLE?

"I lower my voice when I'm unsure of myself, as if that will stop me from saying something too stupid. Sometimes, I wear my glasses to hide behind them. I think my eyes give me away. Maybe wearing glasses will help me hide those windows to my soul. The more hurt I get, the more walls I build around my heart. But the walls harm relationships. It's hard to talk in social events when I don't feel comfortable."

QUESTION: PERSONIFY YOUR FEAR: WHAT DOES IT LOOK LIKE TO YOU? DESCRIBE IT AS THOUGH IT WERE A PERSON IN YOUR LIFE.

"What is fear? Fear to me is like an upset stomach. A shaking, out of control body. Scared eyes, wide eyes. Fear is loss of control. Fear is big. It's consuming, it drowns and tires like water rapids. It consumes, covers the head, keeps one fighting for the top for just one more breath. Allows for that one breath, enough to keep one alive, but makes the body and all its fighting abilities tire and eventually fail. Surrendering to the fight, giving up. At the end of the fight, one floats to the top, gasping quietly. Too tired to try, but floating up enough to breathe and not die. To stop fighting is to live. Fighting makes you sink as though in quicksand. Fear is consuming, overpowering, stronger than me, manipulative, big."

QUESTION: WHY DO YOU HIDE TRUTHS ABOUT YOUR LIFE, LIKE DISAPPOINTMENTS?

"I don't want anyone to know I'm happy about something because if it eventually doesn't go right, they'll find out I'm disappointed. Being open was never a big part of my life. I've never found it easy to talk about sex, relationships, and feelings. I find it hard to be open about anything that hurts me. I guess because it shows faults and imperfections."

Gaining Insight

Finally talking through my anxiety problem with a counselor gave me insights that helped me understand myself. There was a pattern with my past relationships. There were additional risks to the relationship not working out beyond the normal risks. Three of them, including Kirk and that first boyfriend I had an attack over, moved away. I always knew that threat existed when I liked them. One guy had a heart problem and had a heart attack by age twenty; I always worried about his health. Another guy was considering the priesthood, a lifestyle that clearly would prevent him from getting married. Another boyfriend struggled with what it meant to be faithful. These risks went beyond the normal risks any relationship absorbs. I liked these guys, but I couldn't handle the parts of them that increased my chances of being rejected or abandoned.

Examining this helped me understand some of my anxieties. I never believed men would stick around when I needed them; I believed they'd always walk away. Because of these insecurities, I consciously avoided guys who were involved with dangerous careers such as the military, police work, and firefighting.

I also learned through counseling that when we stop our emotions from coming out normally, they come out physically. My counselor had to remind me that crying is acceptable; it is not a sin. It's not a cause for embarrassment; it's necessary to relieve stress. When I would try to stop myself from crying in front of her, she reminded me counseling is safe. You know how much energy it takes not to cry?

She also encouraged me to take the time to feel the pain of a breakup, so I could get over it then move on. I had stuffed down any pain I felt over Nathan and concentrated on fixing my problem. I didn't even know how to deal with the grief of that loss, but it was a loss. It was a relationship I'd been hoping for, for over two years. I shoved the pain away, distracting myself with all these other issues. Putting off feeling that grief only prolonged the healing process. That contributed to why I felt anxiety around him long after the end of our relationship.

Anxiety — A Sin?

This question merits further discussion, probably because it gets under my skin. My counselor suggested I explore the questions, "Is there a sinful side of anxiety? Consider what the Bible says about being anxious. Do you feel guilty for having anxiety? Is it a sign of a lack of faith? Prayer? Sin?"

There are two sides to this. First: Is it a sin to be anxious? Second: Is anxiety caused by anything sinful that we do?

My counselor posed that if the Bible tells us not to be anxious about anything (Philippians 4:6), and I was still anxious, did that make me disobedient? Well, adding that guilt to what's already such a challenging problem does no one any good. Yet the Bible is not going to tell us to do something that's impossible. Instead, I use this verse as encouragement that it's possible to not be anxious. I pray for God's grace to get me there. The Bible doesn't say "fear not" continually for nothing. It's not setting us up for the impossible so we can feel guilty for not being fearless.

For anyone to imply that I did anything "wrong" to bring this ugly problem into my life pushed my buttons. It was difficult to look at personal responsibility. No, I did not initiate this problem. I did reach a point where I realized that by allowing anxiety to continue to rule my life, I was contributing to my on-going struggles. It seemed easier to resort to blaming than to admit I had a role in my response.

An important step toward my healing was to ask God to reveal His truths about the sinful side of anxiety. I believe the answer will be different for each individual situation.

Ezekiel contains references to God allowing His rebellious people to feel panic and fear. He assured Ezekiel, His faithful prophet, that he did not have to be afraid (Ezekiel 2:6). But God said there was panic and not joy among His people because of their sinfulness (Ezekiel 7:7). God also said they would look for peace and not be able to find it (Ezekiel 7:25). Clearly, their sin brought fear into their lives. Therefore, it can't hurt to reflect on whether sin is getting in your way, bringing fear with it.

Any sin leaves a door open for the enemy to get a foothold. Have you left a door open that you didn't mean to open? Could it have anything to do with why panic persists in your life? Have you so deeply identified with panic that it has become a part of you that you are reluctant to release? All of these questions will not necessarily apply, but it's worth asking these questions no matter how challenging they are to answer.

Benefits of Anxiety

My counselor asked me a very important question. I am going to suggest you go through the same exercise:

> **ASSIGNMENT:**
> **Write a list of all the benefits you have in your life because you have this problem.**

I know. You probably think I'm crazy for asking you to do this. It's an amazing exercise. Don't skip it! I realized I did receive some benefits in my life because of panic. Once I thought about it, I was able to come up with a list that gave me comfort. To follow is one of my journal entries about this:

> *Cheryl's Journal (April 1996)*
> *My counselor told me to think about the good side of anxiety. It's an interesting thought. Has anxiety helped me in any way? Is there anything I can be thankful for, for having this problem in my life? One benefit would be my life's passion — writing. Maybe I wouldn't have that love if it weren't for the time I spent facing this problem on paper. My anxiety problems have also kept me from flippantly getting into relationships with guys. I haven't casually dated. While it would have been nice to be normal like everyone else, I do*

believe I was spared some degree of pain by not jumping in and out of relationships. This problem has also kept me dependent on God. I pray and journal more during a relationship than at any other time in my life. My problem reminds me of Paul's thorn that kept him dependent on God.

Part of me wonders if I would have been a writer had certain trials not happened in my life. Writing substituted for talking about how I felt. I didn't have a counselor for a long time. I was too embarrassed by my problem to tell people. Even if I did talk, no one knew what to say to me. I had nowhere to turn except the blank page. And now, writing is my profession. In a way, I feel this experience shaped me into who I am. Writing is one of my favorite activities!

I came up with other benefits as well. I mentioned that it was good I didn't jump in and out of painful relationships. To be honest, I'm also thankful it contributed to me saving myself — intimately — for my husband. While I always firmly believed that was the right and best way to handle sexuality — God's way — I can't say that my faith was the only reason I never gave into sex before marriage. My fear played a role in that. I'm thankful for that, even though my fears needed to be healed.

The final benefit I pinpointed is this book. I consider trials I face on this earth worth it if I am able to reach out and help other people. Writing this book has somewhat redeemed those experiences.

If you reflect on this question, you also will be able to find some benefits in having this challenge in your life, even if it's just that you can reach out to others like yourself with understanding. Do you have friends in your life that you've met because of this common bond? Have you been able to help someone because you understand him or her? Keep digging, and you'll find some gem to be thankful for!

Counseling Alternatives

If you are unable to see a counselor, try to set up a regular time with a trusted mentor to discuss what you're going through. Assign yourself journal questions to discuss each time.

Take your time with the questions in this chapter and discuss your answers with your mentor. Consider finding someone else who shares a similar struggle and act as each other's counselor. Even with the same struggle, you can find objectivity as someone else shares his or her story.

> **ASSIGNMENT:**
>
> **Imagine you are a counselor. A woman who has your particular struggle comes into your office for help. What questions would you ask about her disorder? Her life? Her past? What areas do you feel would be important to discuss? Write down that list of questions. Consider answering them.**

Communion With God Ministries has a wonderful book and tape series called *Counseled by God*. It details how to use God as your Wonderful Counselor. It works!

Look at the way God counseled Jeremiah in his first chapter. (This is one of my favorite counseling sessions in the Bible.) God addressed Jeremiah's fears and insecurities with encouragement, promises, instruction, plus He gave Jeremiah a special anointing to speak. The fact that God was speaking to Jeremiah so directly helped. He spoke through words and pictures.

God will speak to your heart if you'll reach out to Him and listen for His guidance. I will share how God counseled me through depression in Chapter 11.

Trouble At Home

When I started counseling, I was renting a room from my parents and saving up for my big move to the West Coast. I still hadn't told them why my relationship with Nathan fell apart. From my point of view, it was because of my inability to have the relationship without anxiety attacks. Actually, I hadn't even told them I knew I had an anxiety disorder. I didn't want to tell them I was in counseling!

All of this secretiveness was draining; it showed in my moods against them. I was withdrawn. When I did see them, I acted more like a detached boarder than their daughter. I stayed away as much as I could. I didn't think they'd understand what I was doing and why; I wanted to hide it from them. I guess I was continuing the unhealthy pattern I'd had as a teenager—hiding everything. However, this time, I could no longer hide my anger. I felt so much pressure inside that I was about to explode. A couple of months after I had started therapy, they confronted me about the changes they'd seen in my attitude toward them; they rightfully wanted to know where it was coming from and why.

When they asked what was going on, I just broke down. As you well know by now, that was not a normal thing. I never cried in front of them (or anyone else, hardly, except my best friend, Lisa. She was about the only one who'd seen the real and vulnerable me by that point in my life.)

I finally admitted to my parents that I was in therapy and why. I told them how this problem had followed me into adulthood. (The only time they knew I was getting sick over a guy was with Kirk when I was fourteen years old. I never told them it happened with Greg, Nathan, and others.)

My problem wasn't their fault, but I was acting like it was, taking it out on them through my moods. If I had just told them to begin with, I never would have exploded this way. I could say that about my whole life. If I hadn't been so driven toward perfection and so secretive with my faults, I would have been much further along in my life and emotional maturity by this point.

I think it was hard for my parents to understand what I was doing because I had kept them in the dark for so long about my problem. To them, this had come out of nowhere. It was a challenging time for us.

No part of this journey is easy. We can make it through with the wise counsel of God and others, facing questions, facing harsh truths. I don't know where I'd be today if I hadn't gone through counseling. I don't know where I'd be if I hadn't faced the one question I never wanted to face:

The day my counselor asked, "Have you ever been molested?"

CHAPTER 6
Clearing Roadblocks:
Travel Through the Past

A five-year-old girl loved to play in her neighborhood. She and her friends Amy and Matty loved to call the place Happy Town. Happy Town bloomed flowers in springtime, yielded snow during winter, perfect for their sleds and saucers. Their active imaginations molded them into Luke and Leah, the Bionic Woman and Six Million Dollar Man. They were an invincible group.

Or were they?

On days when Amy and Matty couldn't come out to play, the young girl would wander around Happy Town by herself. Riding her bike. Jumping rope. Skipping hopscotch. Belting out her favorite songs. After all, the five-year-old was quite a singer, so she believed.

A guy from the neighborhood watched the young girl play. Some days, he'd ask to join her. She enjoyed the special attention from someone who was older. She must have been special, chosen; he didn't give this attention to her other friends.

Especially not in "that" way.

He would touch her. The little girl wondered if this was wrong. Should she ask her parents? But the guy said it should stay their little secret.

She did stay silent a couple of times.

Then one day, the little girl felt something wasn't right. She decided not to listen to the guy anymore and go to her parents.

Nervously, she approached them. They weren't looking at her, but rather into the bathroom mirror. They must have been getting ready to go out or something.

She blurted the truth out to them. In her own way. She told them something about this guy. They didn't answer her. She stood there a moment. She waited. When they didn't respond, she was left wondering if what happened was right or wrong. She left the room confused, not having gotten an answer to her question. She believed what happened to her was no big deal.

This is by far the hardest chapter to write, the hardest one for me to know other people will read. Panic may appear to come out of nowhere. However, often, it can be traced back to events before panic's beginning.

This was the hardest part of my recovery — talking about what I wanted to forget.

As a young kid, I was molested by someone who lived in my neighborhood in Massachusetts. It was rather confusing for me because I wasn't sure if it was right or wrong. Of course, this person told me it was right. I was special and chosen, wasn't I? If that were true, why did I feel so lousy about it? Or, sometimes, so afraid? I had no idea at the time those encounters would alter the rest of my life, change the way I could relate to men once I was old enough to date them.

There is a big difference between what actually happened that day in the bathroom when I told my parents and my perception of what happened. Allow me to explain.

I believed, for years, that when I told my parents I was being molested, they chose not to answer me or talk about it. I thought this meant what happened was unimportant. It sent a message to my five-year-old mind that if they didn't think it was important, I wouldn't either. I decided not to care. I walked away with the belief that what happened was acceptable and didn't matter.

But it did matter.

It would be twenty years before I would realize the impact that sexual abuse had on my life and my relationships with men.

The reason the abuse stopped is that I told my fellow Happy Town inhabitants, Amy and Matty, the two other five-year-olds, what the guy was doing to me.

One day, they both saw him walking down our street. They ridiculed him right in front of me, yelling at him for what he was doing. Humiliated, I denied it right away, pretending they were lying, pretending I hadn't told.

Regardless, my five-year-old friends rescued me that day. The guy must have gotten scared off when he realized I'd opened my mouth; he never came back.

I went for a long time never mentioning the abuse to anyone. After all, it didn't matter, right? So, why should I care about it? At least that's the message I kept feeding myself. It's unfortunate that I believed that lie for so long.

Warning Signs

There were so many signs I could have picked up on that should have told me the abuse mattered. As an aspiring writer, I always wrote stories, monologues, skits, plays, and poems. The themes of many of those were sexual abuse. I never noticed how preoccupied I was, writing about that issue. It wasn't until years later—when I went through all the material I'd written—that I saw the common theme. It's hard for me to imagine that I used to write stories about girls being abused for *fun*. Since I also enjoyed acting, I liked to act out dramatic monologues about girls relaying their horrific experiences. Obviously this wasn't normal, but I didn't know that. I thought it was just part of my interest in writing and acting, privately playing the drama queen.

In public, I liked to keep up this persona of being in control, especially of my emotions. The only time I enjoyed crying was playing other characters. However, I never wanted my audience to know any of my pain was real.

Allow me to share just one excerpt from a story. One day, my friend Wendy came over and we thought it would be fun to work on a story together. We were thirteen years old. It's hard for me to imagine now why we wanted to write this. Facing what I now know about myself, I understand why I always migrated toward these themes:

> "He mauled her tender breasts viciously before reaching down and unzipping her jeans. He barely paused to tear her panties from her tiny waist. Holding her struggling body beneath his, he quickly undid his own jeans. His face was one of lust as he took her. She felt as if she was split down to the core, both physically and emotionally. After several unbearably long and painful moments, he withdrew from her and went away, leaving her torn, battered form lying limply on the cold hard ground."

I'm not sharing that for the sake of being graphic; I'm using it as an example. This is hardly normal material for healthy thirteen-year-olds to write. I wish at that age I had realized that what happened to me, as a five-year-old, did matter. I cried out with my writing, but I wasn't showing it to anyone with any authority to help me. No one who could help me heard those cries because I hid my writing from the adults in my life. My friends just thought I was dramatic; they got into to act of writing this material as well.

There are countless short stories, skits, and plays I wrote that were about sexual abuse, their titles: *Hidden Scars, A Time to Cry, Secrets, Only Time Will Tell.*

There were other signs throughout my adolescence that should have shown me I needed help. I used to laugh at my mother for crying during television shows. (She would even cry during *The Brady Bunch*. Remember the episode where Marcia gets Mike nominated for Father-of-the-Year? A real tearjerker.) It cracked me up to think anyone would cry watching TV.

Then it happened to me. One night when I was thirteen, I was babysitting. The kids were in bed (which is where anyone you're babysitting should be). I turned on an episode of the sitcom *Webster*. Not exactly a show you'd expect anyone to cry during, right? Well, on January 25, 1985, they aired a special episode called *The Uh-Oh Feeling*, written by Madeline and Steven Sunshine.

Webster found out his young friend Beth was being molested by a substitute teacher. The teacher told her not to tell anyone; it would be their little secret. When Beth realized Webster knew the truth, she made him promise not to tell anyone. Webster overheard the teacher say something to Beth that led Webster to believe he may be this teacher's next victim. Webster faked being sick so he wouldn't have to go to school. Webster was also afraid to keep Beth's promise, for fear that something bad would happen to her again. His broken promise rescued Beth from the abuse.

By the end of the episode, the little girl realized that Webster was the best friend she'd ever had because he told. He spoke up. Back then, that episode had me in tears. I didn't understand it. *I'm a cool thirteen-year-old!* I thought. *I don't cry watching television. That's Mom's job!* I wondered why that episode affected me so much.

While I flashed to memories of what happened to me, I didn't make the connection. I thought, *I'm sure that's not why I'm crying. That event didn't matter to me.* Unfortunately, I was alone watching that episode. No one was there to pick up on yet another sign I needed help.

In 2002, seventeen years after the first time I saw that episode of *Webster*, I got a hold of a tape. The detail and dialogue I remembered from that one viewing was incredible. In rewatching, knowing what I now know about how my own abuse affected me, I understand why that episode was so meaningful.

The offender on the episode used the same terminology as my abuser in trying to make it sound innocent—like a game—including the command to keep that game a secret. Beth also was rescued by the intervention of a young friend. Beth's mother's reaction touched me too, as a mom who didn't want to believe something so horrible could happen to her daughter. Webster's mother told Beth's mother that she had called a counselor to come to school and talk to the kids. Beth's mother's initial reaction was anger. She feared this would turn into an embarrassment for her daughter.

I think it's always hard—at first—for parents to accept when something bad happens to their child, especially something they were unable to prevent from happening. The writers of *Webster* did an excellent job of portraying this dilemma realistically. Beth's mother decided to take Beth to school the day the counselor was there when she couldn't get Beth to talk about the abuse herself. The mother finally admitted they had a problem. The counselor talked to the class about good touches and bad touches and the ones that are confusing—the ones that cause the tingle or the "uh-oh feeling" that signals something may be wrong. It also depicted the all-important message for kids that if abuse does happen, it's not their fault.

I talked to one of the producers about this episode. He said they were flooded with letters from parents praising it because its message gave their abused kids the courage to come forward. I wish, like some of those viewers, I had spoken up then. I could have saved myself years of confusion.

In 2007 during the WGA writer's strike, out of the 12,000 Guild members, I got assigned to the same team as Madeline Sunshine, one of the writers of this special episode. It was an emotional day when I walked up to her, toting my picket sign, telling her that I'd wanted to meet her for a long time.

When I told her she wrote something that really helped me, she immediately responded, "Was it *Webster*?" She knew without me having to explain. We were fast friends, sharing a bond through her words that reached out to help me. What she did through that episode is the same thing that encourages me to put my story in a book and many of my other life experiences and pains in scripts.

I had a similar reaction to other shows besides *Webster* when I was a young teen, including an old episode of *Little House on the Prairie* called "Sylvia" about a girl who was raped, the Ted Danson movie, *Something About Amelia*, about incest, and a *Cagney and Lacey* episode about two sexually abused sisters. All the stories in these television dramas stayed with me for years. Even though none of them were duplicates for my situation, they still spoke to me as I watched the young actresses portray what abused girls act like.

In *Something About Amelia*, Amelia runs away from a boy she was dancing with on the dance floor. I immediately identified with her because I had done that same embarrassing move at that party when I was fourteen! My distrust for guys—like hers—kept me from doing normal activities like dancing innocently at a party.

A couple of times when I had anxiety attacks before dates, a small thought would creep into my head: *Is it possible that "thing" that happened when I was five has anything to do with my fear of boys?* But as quickly as the thought crept in, I'd throw it back out. I firmly believed it had nothing to do with it!

To Lie or Not to Lie

When I was twenty-four and finally decided to go see a counselor, I predetermined that if the topic of sexual abuse came up, I would never admit what happened.

Yes, I planned to lie!

I felt convinced that if I told my counselor what happened, she'd blame my entire problem with anxiety and men on that event, and we'd never get to the heart of where the problem came from. I didn't want my counselor distracted by what I saw as meaningless abuse. So, I vowed I'd keep my mouth shut. I was used to doing that already. I also had the belief that since I was molested and not raped, it mattered even less. I knew too many women who'd been through much worse.

Four sessions in, the counselor asked me, "Have you ever been molested?" I cringed at the question. How could she ask me that? I took a moment to think. *How should I answer? Can I lie to my counselor?*

Then—without warning—the tears came.

And came.

The tears answered for me.

I was so embarrassed. Why did an event that was so meaningless from so long ago have the power to make me cry now? Well, perhaps because I'd never cried. Perhaps because I'd never admitted it was a problem. Perhaps because I'd been in denial almost twenty years by that point.

So, I broke my dangerous vow of silence; I admitted the truth to the counselor. Then I said what hurt me most was that when I told my parents, they didn't say anything. They didn't try to protect me. (At least, that's what I had believed my entire life, even though it turned out that I was wrong.) It was such a painful thing to admit.

The counselor asked me why I had never talked to my parents about it since then, to ask why they had remained silent when I told them. I just couldn't. I had the most amazing parents in the world. They must have just made a mistake, a poor judgment call. Certainly, they loved me and if it happened today, they'd do something. I didn't understand why they didn't do anything back then, but to bring it up now would only hurt them unnecessarily. What could they say to me anyway? I believed there was nothing they could say, and it wasn't worth hurting them.

To follow is an entry I wrote in my journal after this counseling session:

Cheryl's Journal (April 2, 1996)

I've always been afraid to discuss this situation because I didn't want it to take the blame for this problem I have — those physical problems in relationships (where adding the physical or intimate element to a friendship changes it from safe to unsafe). But how can that incident be to blame? It's not like someone I trust violated me. It wasn't a family member or someone I looked up to. Why would that make me afraid of guys? But when I told my counselor what happened, I was surprised by how much the situation bothered me.

Vow of Silence

Once my counselor realized there was no way I was going to talk to my parents about this, she engaged me in a couple of painful exercises. No doubt, these were the worst days in counseling.

First, my counselor asked me to talk to a chair, pretend I was five, and tell my parents what happened from that five-year-old perspective.

Then she had me, as an adult, write them a letter that I'd never give them, asking them why they had never answered me when I asked them if what happened was wrong. It was supposed to allow me to ask all those questions I never had had the chance to ask. And even if I wouldn't get any answers, she felt it was a worthy exercise at least to say what I needed to say.

Then I had to write a letter back to me, from the point of view of my parents, guessing what they may say to me in response. It was short; I couldn't figure out what they could say about it, which is exactly why I never wanted to confront them. Personally, I hated doing all of those journal assignments, and I'm not afraid to say so. No one ever said healing through counseling was easy.

Here's a journal entry I wrote after she made me do the *talk to a chair* exercise:

Cheryl's Journal (April 9, 1996)

> *My therapist made me talk to a chair today and ask all the questions I've never been able to ask. I hated doing that. I understand why it's important, but still. It reminds me of doing monologues in acting. The way it made me cry, the world would have thought I was a good actress. But this isn't acting. This is unearthing all the crap I don't want to talk about. I did learn something tonight through doing that assignment. I have a refusal to let myself be mad without feeling intense guilt. I also have a refusal to let myself be a victim. I'm blocked. And until I can learn to do that, I won't get better. But since I can't change the situation that happened in the past, how do I get over it? When can I let it go? Will it ever be gone and not nag at me? Will I ever not wonder about what happened with my parents? Will I ever not wonder if that guy had left me alone, would I not have had this problem my whole life? All these years, I told myself I had no pain about it. Was I better off believing that? Well, obviously not since it came out in physical ways. I wonder if my parents could handle my pain. Is it easier for them to not know? It's like I want so desperately to keep this hidden from them, to spare them. Yet, I resent them for not knowing, for not asking me what's wrong. Yet, I'm the one shutting them out. I keep running the other way, avoiding them so they can't ask. What is wrong with me?*

I wrote that entry during the season I mentioned when I was living with my parents, yet hardly talking to them. The pressures of my anger were building up each day. That day, when they finally asked what was wrong with me, I could only admit I'd started counseling for my panic problem. I couldn't bring myself to tell the truth about the abuse and how that was the cause of it. I couldn't bring myself to ask the questions I always wanted to ask. I wish I had at that point! I probably could have healed a lot sooner. It would be six more years until I would find the courage to do so. (Okay, so I'm a little slow.)

Once the abuse was out in the open with my counselor, she encouraged me to take the time to be a victim since I'd never let myself be one back then. Well, that didn't sound like fun to me! I told her I was concerned if I let myself, I would never be able to climb back out of that. She said I had to take the time to admit what happened, admit its impact, and take the time to be the victim I never was before. Here's a journal entry I wrote after my counselor suggested that:

> *Cheryl's Journal (April 9, 1996)*
> *I don't remember ever crying about it. Not even back when it all happened. Not when I told my parents in that bathroom doorway. Not when nothing was said. I never really got upset. I was just confused. I've always felt that so many others had it a lot worse. I shouldn't dwell on it, think about it, or feel bad about it. It just shouldn't bother me. At least that's what I've always told myself.*

My counseling ended after six months of talking through these issues. She told me to come back once I started dating again. Walking back into the dating scene was furthest from my mind. I just wanted to be normal for a while. I wasn't convinced I was better just because I'd finally started talking about it.

With or Without Cause

If you are unable to pinpoint any direct cause of your anxiety problems, you can still heal. Even if you do find the cause, it doesn't mean the problem will suddenly go away. It will help you understand yourself better. I know for me, understanding where I was coming from made it a lot easier for me to face my problem and forgive myself for having one.

Christa Sands, a woman I met in a screenwriting program, wrote the book *Learning to Trust Again* about her experience of being sexually abused. Her words resonated so deeply with my experience. She went through the same types of challenges, including years of silence. To follow is an excerpt from her book:

> "In that first moment of abuse he violated not only my body but also the very depths of my being. In an instant he broke the trust I had with him and with all men.... I felt dirty and embarrassed, certain that if others found out what happened they would be disgusted with me. I had to hide, but where? Unconsciously I decided the only safe place for me was far down inside myself. No one could hurt me there. No one could see how awful I was. Deep roots of shame began to choke my soul. I retreated to my inner world and wore a mask to cope with the outer world.... One of the main ways I coped was by pushing away anyone who dared come too close. I distanced myself from most people and social situations... Within the protective shell that became my own prison I lived a safe but lonely existence, longing for the one thing too risky to pursue—close relationships.... Victims of abuse unconsciously use defense mechanisms to survive, to protect themselves from emotional pain." (1)

Is your anxiety disorder your way of protecting yourself from any abuse you've endured? It's a tough question, but it must be asked. It must be faced, head-on. Trust me. Facing it is worth it!

Work your way through the pain to get to the other side where the light can bring life back into your world. Light comes through truth, not hidden secrets. One of the most important points Christa makes in her book is, "We must find hope in the fact that healing and wholeness are not only possible but worth the journey through pain." (2)

ASSIGNMENT:

If you have no idea where your panic problem came from, go through old journals if you have any. Look for elements that may give you clues about what may have brought this on. They may also reveal previous times you experienced anxiety without realizing that's what was going on. If you ever wrote stories or poems, or if you gravitated toward particular types of books, movies, television shows, or songs, scour those for common themes.

Knocking Down Barriers

Have you been blaming God for your disorder, for allowing it to plague your life? Have you blamed another person?

If I wanted to, I could blame my abuser. I could live in a place of bitterness against him for all that I suffered because of his depravity. Instead, I chose to heal. I wanted his power over my life to end. I knew my heart needed to heal. My heart needed to release any tie to him that would keep his affect on my life in the present. Gripping anger tightly wasn't going to get me to a place of true healing. Facing it and then moving on would. This meant I had to forgive him, even in the face of knowing the lasting effects of what he did to me. How long I floundered! How many relationships my fear-filled reactions shipwrecked!

By this point, it had been twenty years since the abuse, fourteen years of struggling to date guys. That is hard to forgive! Yet, I knew I had to so I could get my life back. I had to forgive for my sake, not his.

One night I prayed, "Lord, I think I forgive him. But how do I forgive someone so long after the events happened when I hardly remember him? I remember who he was, but not what he looked like. Lord, it's like I'm trying to forgive some intangible person."

Sometimes, when we pray, God answers right away. I was sitting on my bed. As soon as that last sentence left my lips, this guy's face flashed across my memory! I was filled immediately with disgust. I didn't hate him, but I was angry. It was easy to say I forgave him before this point—before I had his face smack in front of me! I still had some forgiving to do. I prayed through it, asking God for His grace.

Thankfully, it wasn't long after that prayer I forgot the details of the face. God gave it to me long enough to forgive. Then, He divinely erased the image so the perpetrator could remain a faceless memory. He no longer has any power to influence, control, or hurt me.

Much later in my walk with God—when I was in my early thirties—God started to speak to me and counsel me through dreams. God sent me several beautiful dreams that were instrumental in sealing this healing over the sexual abuse. One I call a "deliverance dream" because I felt released of all evil pressures that had come into my life as a result of the abuse—pressures like shame, embarrassment, demeaning thoughts against myself, fears of men, and fears of intimacy.

God also sent me a dream where I faced the adult version of this abuser. In the dream, I chose to stop running away from him, turn around, and face him. Even though I recognized his face, I wasn't afraid. I knew he had no power to hurt me anymore. When I woke up from both of those dreams, I was so excited! I felt completely freed from all the past pain and fear. I thank God and praise Him for taking such great care in healing me this way.

Unforgiveness is always a barrier to healing. God walked me systematically through forgiving everyone I needed to forgive in this situation. It didn't happen all at once. It took me years to walk through each step of forgiveness. Forgiving the offender was only the beginning.

Breaking the Silence

I wish I would have plunged right in and rooted it all out during that one year in 1996. If I'd cleaned it all up then, I could have moved on with my life!

I didn't.

I was still too afraid to try dating again and still too afraid to talk to my parents about what had happened. It took me many more years to break my silence with them. It was both the hardest and best thing I ever did. Breaking down the walls of perfection and becoming vulnerable were huge strides down my road toward healing.

I had already been well into working on this book. I knew I couldn't publish something like this without telling this part of my story. I didn't want my parents to read about what they supposedly did or didn't do in book form. I knew I had to be brave and face them. What I didn't realize was how important that step would be to my healing and to strengthening my relationship with them.

By this point, I lived in California. I went to visit them for Christmas. The day I decided I had to break the silence was filled with much anxiety. Gratefully, I did not have a panic attack.

Maybe that's because I chickened out.

How could I do this to them? How could I dig up all that pain? I went to bed frustrated with myself for not being brave enough. The next night, I knew I had to do it! If I were ever going to get the chance to help other people through my story, I had to speak up. Otherwise, there would be no book to publish. I would have written all of this for myself.

I sat my mother down late one night. There was no way I could have handled that talk with both parents at the same time. I tried to be subtle at first, asking if she ever wondered where my anxiety problems with guys came from. I asked if she ever had any theories; she didn't. She knew it was a little abnormal for me to get sick every time Kirk would come pick me up, but she never saw a direct cause. I kept hoping I could get her to say it so I wouldn't have to, but that wasn't working.

Finally, I blurted it out. Did she realize that my panic disorder started because that guy in our neighborhood had molested me?

Imagine my surprise when she said she had no idea that had ever happened to me. I asked her why she was acting surprised. After all, I told my parents when it happened. My mother had no recollection of me ever stepping into that bathroom doorway and telling her and my father what was going on. She did, however, remember a phone call from the mother of my friend, Matty. Matty's mother warned mine to keep an eye out for that guy because it was possible he was abusing me. Matty must have told his mother what I told him.

My parents discussed the phone call and felt I would have said something to them if anything were going on. They didn't want to scare me by asking, in case it wasn't true. They decided to watch, to wait and see if this person came around. Yet, he never came back. This timed out with Amy and Matty scaring the guy off in the street. So, when my parents never saw him around, they assumed nothing had happened.

I described the scene in the bathroom to my mother, the day I believed I told her and my father. She said based on what I described, how they appeared to be getting ready to go out, they must not have been listening to me. Surely, if they had, they would have done something about it.

That part of my memory just never made sense to me, knowing all my life how much they loved me. At the time, it just seemed like I was being ignored. My mother believes that whatever I told them must not have sounded like what I was really saying or they would have paid attention. I can understand that. As a five-year-old, I wouldn't have known the right words to use, like abuse or molestation. Who knows what I said that day? (And if you'd known me back then, I was a major chatterbox. No one in the world could have possibly listened to and absorbed every word I said. In fact, on road trips, they used to try to entice me with the "Silent Game" because I was so chatty.)

So, imagine my surprise in finding out after twenty-five years of silence that the situation was not as I had perceived. It's unfortunate that it happened the way it did. Maybe I could have gotten help sooner. Maybe I would have understood that what happened did matter, so I wouldn't have gone through so many years having no clue what was wrong with me.

I can honestly say, even though as a teen I showed signs of having issues with sexual abuse, there's no way my parents would have known. I never let them see my plays, my stories, my endless tales of girls being abused. Those were saved for my friends only. I also developed a pattern of only talking to my friends about my problems because I wanted to appear capable and independent to my parents.

My view of what really happened was way off; it took a long time for me to find that out. I experienced lots of pain and anger against my parents unnecessarily. What it took to heal was breaking that silence!

Right away, my mother was supportive. She offered books, tapes, websites, anything she thought would be helpful toward my inner healing. She tried to do everything she didn't have the chance to do before. She supported my desire to write a book to help other people.

I was too afraid to have that conversation with my father. My father and I have this amazing bond; we're buddies. He's always on my side, always there to help me pick out the best computer, the best car, the best whatever. (He gets more excited when I'm shopping for something new than I do. He's adorable!)

We had just finished working together on a script of his father's life, where we were this fun little team interviewing survivors of a big mining disaster. How could I wreck that by digging this stuff up?

For some reason, it was too difficult for me. So, I made my mother tell him about our conversation. And still, it was tough for us to talk about all of this. I didn't want our relationship to stop being fun. I didn't want to face the pain with him. I didn't want him to feel helpless. I knew hearing about something he couldn't change would do that. Yet, I had to speak up. And you know what? We survived it. Now, my father and I have a wonderful relationship that is far more open than it's ever been.

I can only imagine how awful it was for my parents to find out all of this so much later in my life, knowing there isn't anything they can do to change what happened long ago.

Just getting it out in the open has been healing for me and for my family. It was the first step for me to be able to relate to them as a real human being. I could finally tell them when I had real problems with real ups and downs, emotionally. It was the first time I stopped pretending, the first time I let them be there for me emotionally through something that brought me real pain. Finally, I wasn't hiding.

My mother asked me if I believed I would not have had a panic problem if they had been able to do something about the abuse back then. I believe I would still have had the same problem. Sexual abuse is about broken trust. Getting justice wouldn't have restored that. The only difference it could have made is I would have gotten help much sooner. I may not have spent twenty years denying it had any impact.

I would like to encourage anyone who's been through anything like this to be open. Talk about it; don't pretend it didn't matter. Don't get in the habit of being secretive. It only hurts you. You will heal quicker if you're open. That is far more important than the embarrassment you may experience when admitting hurts.

I had so much anger that I held inside for so long. If I'd spoken up sooner, I would have known that what I believed about that situation and my parents' reaction to it was wrong. I would have trusted them more, been willing to get their perspective on my problems while I was growing up. Instead, I depended on my peers. My friends didn't necessarily have the best answers about life. They were my age! I'm sorry I missed going to my parents back then.

Thankfully, that has completely changed in the present. Now I know how to say to them, "This hurts." I feel no embarrassment about that. I have no trouble crying in front of them. Their emotional support has been amazing to me.

I do recognize that not everyone will receive the support I did from family. Sometimes, bringing up this stuff can cause additional pain for those in families who are unable to support one another through these types of challenges. This is especially common if a person causing pain is within one's own family. I can only hope those in this situation can find support from other family members or a church family.

Don't let the fear of other's reactions keep you from coming forward; otherwise, truly healing may not ever be possible. If the person you want to confront is in your own family, be sure not to handle it alone. Seek God about the best way to deal with the situation, and ask Him and trusted mentors for guidance.

Let's Talk About Sex

Once I finally faced the fact the abuse was the cause of my extreme fear of men, I had to face the ugly truths that came with it. Yes, I feared rejection, abandonment, and a lack of acceptance—all the standard anxiety disorder fears.

I couldn't ignore my other real fears: fears of intimacy, fears of sharing on an emotional level with a man, and sex. It's no coincidence that for several of my scenarios I was able to keep friendships with guys, without panicking. Then, the moment it went beyond friendship, I'd freak out. (Greg and Nathan are two such examples.) I could handle regular, nonphysical friendships with them. But once the relationship moved to dating, panic gripped me.

It's like panic was the friend that thought she was protecting me from getting too close physically. (I mean, really, how can you kiss a guy while you're throwing up?) Neither of these guys were a danger to me, of course. Neither one was pressuring me for sex, but I still had to face my fear of intimacy. That is not easy for me to admit. But, hey! This is about truth, right? (Insert my beet red face here.)

Once I settled into a new relationship, I was able to share some degree of intimacy. (That was usually around the time my relationships ended—story of my life!) I did have a few scattered circumstances throughout my life where I found someone to kiss who didn't cause me much anxiety. That was usually a fluke—usually with someone I felt attracted to but had no emotional attachment. That always surprised me when I felt calm.

Once I made the connection between my anxiety disorder and the abuse, I could forgive myself for having these fears. It's common for abuse victims. Once I started telling a few friends about this experience, I was surprised to find how many had also been abused and had struggled with anxiety with men.

For years, I didn't know how to deal with this fear. I figured it was easier to just not date. I waited over five years after Nathan to try again. I'll share that story in Chapter 8.

Breaking Through Barricades

One helpful study I recommend is Mark and Patti Virklers's book and seminar tape series *Prayers That Heal the Heart.* It specializes in having people go back to a time when they were hurt and visualizing what Jesus was doing when that happened. Restructuring how one sees an event can be instrumental in healing that bad memory. This healing was vital. Abuse leaves one feeling unloved, not treasured, not protected. I felt damaged, felt I'd never be accepted "as is" by anyone. Prayer and God's intervention were the only ways I could heal from this.

Another helpful book my mother gave me was *Ancient Paths* by Craig Hill. It deals with thinking about the past and how it affects your present, then moving beyond it.

I want to be clear: I do not advocate blaming the past for our problems. We can change how we feel about something if we're willing to let God heal us and speak to our hearts. Yes, bad things happen; that's universal. The only control we have is how we react to those painful events now. There is a huge difference between identifying the blows we sustained that contributed to our problems versus using our so-called right to continue to blame someone or ourselves. Blame involves choosing not to forgive. Blame keeps us angry and bitter.

God has not given us the right to harbor grudges and grievances against others, no matter how wrong they were. Once you identify causes, only ponder them long enough to recognize the hurts. Then, move past them swiftly into a place of forgiveness. Continue to forgive each time those old thoughts creep back up. This is for your own good and your own healing.

I do not place blame for my problems on my abuser, on my parents, or on myself. I know what happened to me was not my fault. I don't have to keep panic in my life. I can choose to keep it if I want to play the blame game and keep holding onto the bad. But I don't! Blaming doesn't help me heal. Identifying the source of the initial blows was important. Then, I had to move on. Thankfully, our God is strong enough to heal us from that place of pain when we're willing to reach out to Him and let Him do a good work in us.

Do you feel you need to forgive someone for your disorder? Did someone do something to you that you believe is the cause? Ask God to show you what you need to forgive. God will answer. He will supply the next step, but it's still our job to take the first one.

God's work has required much fire—refining, purifying, painful fire— as I had to face everything I never wanted to face. God is a God of truth and He blows the walls off any lies we choose to hold onto, any hurts we are unable or unwilling to face. God has been with me through every ounce of pain: the day of the abuse, the day I tried to get help, the days I wanted to kill myself. He has never left my side.

If anyone knows pain and suffering, it's Christ, who walked on this earth and suffered vast physical pain and abuse. He understands my pain even more than I do. Inviting Him not only to become my Savior and Lord of my life—but to come forth as my Wonderful Counselor—has been vital to my healing. Jesus is healing me. I just had to meet Him halfway. The journey so far has been a walk with Jesus, even when I kicked and screamed, cried and blamed. Jesus took it all!

My journey took a large leap forward with this important step. But it wasn't over yet.

CHAPTER 7
Cleansing Rain:
Healing Through Writing

The Mask — a poem (1985)
I wish this world were different,
That people would not hurt each other,
That they would be themselves,
And not be masked by a cover.
They sometimes say they're one thing,
But turn out as something else.
The deception they present,
To hide the hurt they've felt.
I love when people unmask,
And just become themselves,
And not put on an act,
Problems to others they tell.
(Cheryl McKay)

This is the fun chapter; this is where we get to frolic on the playground of creativity. As you know, I've been promoting right-brain, creative activities, and heart languages since the beginning of this book. This is a fun chapter because I am a creative writer at heart. I had no idea when I was younger that creativity tapped into my heart that needed healing. Some things I wrote were downright silly, but I sure had fun writing them! I hope you'll jump in with me here and open your creative mind.

There are so many creative activities that can help you deal with your anxiety. These activities include writing, acting, singing, music, painting, drawing, and just about any form of artistic expression. This chapter will primarily focus on writing. I'll discuss journaling, short stories, poems, monologues, scenes, and scripts. I wrote all of these throughout my journey.

There was one year I wrote ten plays. Every single one dealt with issues teen girls were facing. I loved investing in the dramatic life of a teen I created on paper. Through those characters, I was able to feel emotions I couldn't express. As I mentioned in the previous chapter, my issues with guys and anxiety came out in stories and scenes. I found it healing to write scenes that said what I always wished I could say out loud. I could even act them out in the privacy of my own room. No one had to know: it was just between my mirror and me.

I loved when I could cry because it made me feel like I was a good actress. I had no idea that when I let myself do that, baby steps toward healing were taking place. My emotions needed that healthy outlet. I enjoyed playing the role of the tragic teenager. I wasn't a good actress onstage; but in the privacy of my own room, I gave Oscar-worthy performances.

Create Your Characters
To follow are four creative writing assignments:

CREATIVE ASSIGNMENT #1:
Write a scene that depicts your life. Write the role you wish you weren't playing, depicting your anxious self. Dramatize it. Exaggerate your story. Write a scene Julia Roberts would kill to play because she'd win another Oscar. Write the people in your lives the way you see them. Consider writing a scene leading up to an attack as well as a

scene when an attack happens. Then, if you want to have a little fun with it, act out the scene in the privacy of your own home.

CREATIVE ASSIGNMENT #2:

Is there a character you want to be? How about a person free from anxiety, a person doing and saying all the things you wish you could do or say? Write that scene. Create that character. Give him or her a name you like. Put the character in situations where you've panicked in the past, only write the success. Write the version of the story you wish you could play in real life. Write a dialogue between that character and someone else. This can be a person in your life or a fictional person. (I liked to write about gorgeous, long-haired guys taking me out on anxiety-free dates, kissing me passionately.) Act this scene out privately; really get into the role. (Well, except the kissing passionately part.) It may be awkward at first, but try to get into the scene.

You can use this experience later when you find yourself in the same situation in real life. Later, you can tap into how empowered you felt when you were acting out the anxiety-free version of the scene. Role-playing a scene where you don't have your usual panic attack can help build your confidence.

You can first try this exercise alone. When you're comfortable, consider inviting a trusted friend to play the other person in the scene. It doesn't all have to be written out. You can also improvise. Write out a scenario, then, make up the dialogue as you go along. (I promise this can be fun! All recovery assignments don't have to be serious!)

CREATIVE ASSIGNMENT #3:

Write a monologue from your point of view of the words you would use to tell someone for the first time about your anxiety struggles. You can write this like your personal story. It may help you in future situations when you have to tell someone for real. The more I told people my story, the more I got used to it. It can't hurt to practice at home.

Another approach could be to write a monologue you'd want for a dramatic theater audition. Really get into the angst of your story. Then, act it out. (This time, you're trying to win a Tony.)

Write the comic version as well. Yes, you can find comedy when you learn to not take yourself so seriously. Comedy and laughter can be so healing, and they release anxiety. Write it as though you're a stand-up comic, making fun of yourself and your fears. Of course, you don't want to be hurtful to yourself. Just have fun with the fact that you are not perfect. You may remember those funny moments you shared with yourself alone once you're out in public. It may undercut your fear. (No one has to know what's making you smile, what's helping you cope!)

To follow is an example of a monologue I wrote in 1986, depicting my struggle with Kirk, who I mentioned in Chapter 1. I wrote this through the eyes of a character "Samantha" about a guy she liked named Kirk. Changing the names didn't change who it was about, as you'll see it's rather true to my life. I wrote about it in a much more lighthearted way than I felt.

SAMANTHA: Kirk. Gee. What can I say about Kirk, besides the fact that he's ultra cute? I was so excited when we got paired in drama club to do a scene together. I suggested a scene where he could play my boyfriend. But one day, this girl came to meet him after rehearsal. For some reason, I highly doubted she was his sister. Hmm. Maybe it's the way she greeted him with, you know, a kiss. If I had a brother, I wouldn't kiss him. Not that way. As soon as they walked out the door, I ran into the bathroom to throw up. Yeah! Not sure where that came from. I hadn't been sick before she walked in and kissed him. I don't think kissing is gross or anything. I just didn't like her kissing my man — one who was no longer mine. Actually, he's not really a man yet either. He's, like, seventeen. The next day, Kirk invited me to go out to eat with him and his girlfriend. Yeah, she was one of those nice ones, welcoming me, not having the first clue I adored her boyfriend! Kirk told me to bring my boyfriend. Newsflash, Kirk! I don't have one! I wanted you! You were mine in my fantasy realm, then, she had to go and wake me up! Oh well. I kept that to myself. I went out with them. And you know what? I had to run away from the table to throw up again! What is wrong with me?

CREATIVE ASSIGNMENT #4:

Write a short story of what it's like for you to go through a panic attack. Write in the first person. Use your inner monologue of what goes on inside your head. (I showed you a sample of this at the beginning of Chapter 2, when I said lovely words to myself like, *What is wrong with me? Why do I do this every time? I'm so stupid. No one else behaves as ridiculously as I do.* Those gentle words.) You will use this inner monologue in Chapter 10 when we rewrite the lies we tell our minds. This monologue can help you pinpoint that stream of junk that flies through your thoughts. Write this as though you're trying to make an outsider understand exactly how you feel—both emotionally and physically—during an attack. Give them a peek into what happens inside your mind.

I hope you'll take the time to try these exercises. Once you get into them, you may even find them fun. I found them freeing. I also found it showed me an outside picture of what I was going through. I could look objectively into the eyes of a character I created. I found I had empathy and understanding when I saw what my characters went through, why they had the problems they did.

Modern Day Poets

Writing poetry can be so healing. Don't feel like it has to rhyme. Write from your heart. Write the "whiny country song" version or the "angry rock" version. To follow are examples of how I wrote about my challenges in the form of poetry. This first one I consider my "Oh-woe-is-me" rock ballad:

When Forever's Just a Lie — a poem (1990)

I look in the mirror and don't like what I see.
But it's my very own life looking back at me.
Words spoken untrue, promises made broken.
How can I go on, when I want my life to end?
All those words you spoke of forever were just to keep me smiling.
You never planned on sticking around; you just held the present moment.
How can I go on when forever's just a lie?
I used to look into your eyes, thinking I saw my future.
You let me believe we had more than we really did.
You held me close and said you loved me when all the time you knew you'd leave.
Now I'm alone with only my memories of a love lost forever.
The loss of one who couldn't accept the imperfect version of me.
But the true me, you never caught a glimpse of.
The true me, you didn't stick around to see.

Maybe When I Die (1986)

I cry out, but no one is there.
I've had so many problems, and no one wants to help.
All they want is to get down my back for everything.
Why do I have to be perfect?

Even on days when I hurt.
They have no mercy.
No cares.
They think only of themselves.
They can't even consider my feelings.
My sorrows.
My problems.
I want to give up.
But it means more to me than that.
But I've had it!
I just don't care!
Don't lie, you do.
But, why?
Why are there problems?
They load up and never go away.
Why is this happening?
There's only one person I can depend on.
Jesus.
If I didn't, I'd probably just give up.
No one else really cares.
I hate life!

While some of what I wrote may have come across as morbid, it was those little outlets that kept me alive.

My Story According to Hollywood

Next, I'd like to share an example of how I used the scriptwriting process in my healing. In 1999, I wrote a fictional screenplay about three generations of women who suffer from anxiety disorders. It's called *Katie's Mountain*. I wrote a story about a twenty-four-year old woman named Katie who had suffered from anxiety attacks around guys her whole life, but she never understood why. When she tries to marry her best friend, Danny, she ends up deserting him at the altar, unaware of what she is so afraid of. The movie explores her search to find the reason she has a panic disorder, while also dealing with her agoraphobic grandmother and her mother, who hides that she also has an anxiety disorder.

Writing this script was my first step in coming forward. It gave me a way to speak up about my challenges without having to say, "This is about me." I could talk through Katie instead. While the screenplay version is fictionalized and separate from my life, writing it was so healing. I felt anxious as I was writing it, but I enjoyed that! It helped me get into Katie's character as deeply as I could. It was hard to write Katie's anxiety attack scenes. I penned her every move, emotion, word, and tear with as much honesty as I could unearth. It was the first big step I made toward learning how to talk about my problem outside private, counseling settings.

The script turned out to be a great tool I could hand people and say, "This is me. Read this, and you'll understand where I'm coming from." You can use your creative writing assignments this way as well. Share them with others who struggle to understand you.

Maybe someday a Hollywood producer will want to help me turn *Katie's Mountain* into a TV movie. But even if that never happens, the process of telling Katie's story did me a world of good. I was able to dramatize many of the feelings I'd stuffed away for years. I felt like that script was a gem in the rough—a script I could be proud of, a script I grew personally through writing. I felt like my lead character became a friend. (And I wished I could write her amazing fiancé into existence!)

To follow are two sample scenes from *Katie's Mountain*. This takes place after Katie had a panic attack and deserted her fiancé at the altar. This is before she realizes she has a panic disorder. This mirrors my journey in that she has reactions to men, but doesn't know what they're called or why she has them.

Scenes from movies are written differently than short stories. Try to imagine it on-screen with actors playing the roles:

SCENE 1: INT. CHURCH BATHROOM — DAY

(Katie is on the floor in the bathroom, having just gotten sick. Her best friend, Regan, kneels down and hands Katie a paper towel. Katie looks at Regan, who seems to understand. Jenna, Katie's mother, clearly doesn't get it.)

JENNA: Katie, what happened?

(Carmen, Katie's was-to-be mother-in-law, pounds on the bathroom door, trying to get in. Katie hears her yelling through the door.)

CARMEN: Get out here right now, Katie!

KATIE: No.

REGAN: You don't have to.

(Katie clutches her head with both hands and rocks back and forth. She closes her eyes and over-breathes.)

REGAN: Slow down. Katie, slow.

(Regan gently tries to move a hand from Katie's head. She's been with Katie through these anxiety attacks before.)

REGAN: Don't fight it.

(With a grunt, Katie puts her hand back where it was.)

KATIE: I'm sinking again, Regan.

REGAN: We're not going to let that happen.

JENNA: Katie, we've got to get out there. Everyone is waiting. We look stupid.

(Regan shoots Jenna a look that screams "shut up.")

REGAN: It's okay to be sick. You're allowed.

CARMEN: Katie, if you don't open the door, I'm going to break it down.

(That does it. At the pushing, Katie throws up.)

SCENE 2: INT. KATIE'S BEDROOM — NIGHT

(It's the night of the truncated wedding. Katie never made it back inside the sanctuary. She's sedated, lays on her bed, numb. Too tired to cry anymore. Katie is startled by a knock on her window. Her loving fiancé, Danny, has climbed up the tree and onto the small roof outside her bedroom. After a beat, she goes to the window and opens it. She stays inside her room. She needs the boundary between them. He just stares at her. His confused, hurt soul pains her.)

KATIE: I want to marry you more than anything.

DANNY: Then why?

KATIE: I don't know.

DANNY: What does that mean?

KATIE: There are things you don't know.

DANNY: I've known you almost your whole life. What else is there?

(Katie opens her mouth to speak, then stops. Her nerves start to come back.)

KATIE: I— I can't.

DANNY: What's changed since last night? Katie, I love you. How could I say it more?

KATIE: Danny, I can't be around you.

DANNY: Are you saying it's over?

KATIE: I don't know.

(Katie slips off her engagement ring and puts it on the windowsill. Katie's dream is slipping away before her. She doesn't know why or how to fix it. She has no choice but to send Danny away.)

I used this script to write a character that was facing all my fears. I had to challenge myself with each draft to be more honest, to dig deeper. It was easy to write a woman's fear of her boyfriend. It was not easy to specify her fear was of intimacy and sex. A trusted mentor, who happened to be a producer interested in this project, had to encourage me to be more honest about my fears of sexual intimacy as I wrote Katie's journey. I resisted at first—embarrassed, afraid. I experienced anxiety trying to add that into the script. Eventually, I prevailed and got it on paper, but it wasn't easy. It was the beginning of me learning how to talk about that part of my fears. Having those fears is common for those who've been sexually abused.

Dearest Friend (or Foe)

Besides writing dramatizations, stories, monologues, scenes, and scripts, you can write letters. This can be with the intention of sending them or not. You decide. You don't even have to decide until after you write the letters. I wrote several in therapy. For example, I wrote one to my abuser. This was not with the intention of sending it.

Is there someone you feel doesn't understand you and you'd like the chance to say what you've been holding back? Is there someone you'd like to confront because of the way they've contributed to your disorder, like an abuser? Write the most honest letter you can. Say exactly what you always wished you could say but didn't have the guts. Later on, if you decide confronting this person is necessary— possibly through a letter—consider getting advice from a trusted mentor. Let someone help you decide if parts of your honest letter should be rewritten first. Never send a letter that could be harmful to you, your safety, or your healing.

I wanted to reach out to someone in my family, but I was too afraid to talk about it in person or on the phone. So, I wrote a letter. I chose to tell my mother's sister, Jackie. In Chapter 8, I will share excerpts from this letter and pieces of her amazing response.

Dear Private Journal

Okay, so my journals are no longer so private, but yours can be. I discussed at length in Chapter 5 how I used a journal throughout counseling. You can also use a journal like a diary. Use it as your safe haven, a place to vent. Writing about what's going on within us can be so therapeutic.

Have you ever tried to explain to someone how you felt and the words just wouldn't come out right? Journaling can help you sort out how you feel about a situation. Writing stuff out first made it easier for me to verbalize my feelings later. Sometimes, if I were in conflict with a person about something, I'd journal my thoughts first. Then, I'd go to the person and tell him or her how I felt.

Sometimes, it helps to go back and read what I've written to track personal growth. I like to read how ridiculous I sound at times. (Yeah, I know, I'm strange.) I've had many eye-opening experiences, reading how hopeless I sounded one day, only to find a much better disposition the next. I was able to learn triggers in the ups and downs of my moods. Track your emotional journey this way.

You can also use a journal as a diary of symptoms and panic triggers. Keep lists of how you feel when the anxiety starts, what brings the feelings on, what happens during attacks, how long they last, and your list of symptoms.

To follow are samples of journal entries:

Cheryl's Journals:

(May 1989)

Everything doesn't last forever. Some seasons last longer than others. You can work so hard trying to accomplish one thing. It may make you feel good about yourself, but it won't always be there. I treasure friendships, but they are ever changing. Nothing remains the same. You can't go back and relive the past — those precious moments tucked away in your memory. Sadly, you can't do it over — better this time. The most valuable part of your past and memories is what you've learned. That's what you've gained. That's what you can take with you. We need to keep moving forward and not hinder the growth of the future.

(December 1995)

When it comes to relationships and personal problems, I become a bumbling idiot. I get tongue-tied, flustered. It's hard for me to express how I feel. I get nervous. I'm much more likely to talk about something if I am asked first. I may want to talk about something, but it's hard for me to bring up the topic. It's like I need probing. Maybe that's because if someone asks a question, I feel more comfortable talking about something personal. Like they're interested enough to want to know the answer. I also have a fear of not being listened to.

(May 1997)

I hate my life. I hear all these things I say to myself like "loser" and "what a freak." I know I'm a workaholic. At least when I'm working, I have an excuse to not be social. It gives me an excuse to not have friends or a boyfriend. I'm a social-phobic. I hate meeting new people. I hate events where I don't know people. I don't connect well. Why am I so weird? I keep people away. I feel lonely; yet, when I'm with people, I just want them to go away. I used to like affection, but now I shrug away. I feel scared and alone. My life is meaningless. I can't seem to get it right. But what is right? My anxiety problems add to my freakish ways. Sometimes, I want to squeeze my head. My skin. I want it off. I don't want to be who I am. No one has any idea of the hell I live in my mind. Some days, I long for purpose. Someday, someone will read this entry and wonder what on earth I'm talking about.

Your journal doesn't have to be all about frustrations and pain. It can also be your playground. Have fun with it. Go out in nature, enjoying God's creation as you journal about your life, about God and His love for you.

To follow are five journal assignments:

JOURNAL ASSIGNMENT #1:
Write out a list of 10 things you really love about yourself. Try not

to list accomplishments here. Try to list positive traits about you and your character — who you are that really defines what makes you unique, what makes you, *you*.

JOURNAL ASSIGNMENT #2:

If you are unhappy with your life, what steps can you proactively take to change it? What steps will take you where you want to go? Make a list of goals and a list of proactive things you can do to improve your life or yourself. Start with small goals at first, then, graduate to bigger ones.

JOURNAL ASSIGNMENT #3:

Think *Freaky Friday*. Consider someone's life you wish you had. What is it about that life you want? Would you take the bad along with it? The problems? Would it be worth it? What do you have in your life that this person probably wishes they had?

JOURNAL ASSIGNMENT #4:

Make a list of ten things that scare you (people, places, events, situations). Then, make a list of ten things that bring you comfort. Are any of those ten comforts ones you can bring into situations that scare you? Can you bring a source of comfort into a source of anxiety? (For example, I mentioned in Chapter 1, when a trusted friend would show up during an attack, sometimes I was able to calm down.)

JOURNAL ASSIGNMENT #5:

Read about all the people in the Bible who experienced fear. How did they handle it? What did they do with their fears? How did they move past their fears? In what ways did God help them, comfort them? Journal about their coping methods.

Generate your own journal assignments. Get creative! Share your journaling with trusted friends and counselors. Use it to track your growth. You will grow through journaling! You will get sick of writing the same complaints. It will motivate you to strive to move past those places, those fears, those complaints. In the Appendix, I've included extensive journal entries during the darkest year of my life.

Write Psalm 151

Journal out your prayers to God. Try writing your prayers as though you are writing a Psalm that God could have published in the Bible. Psalms vary from complaints to prayers to poems of thanksgiving. I love the many examples in Scripture of regular people—like you and me—who poured out their pain to God in written form. Write honestly. Write lyrically, as though writing a song or poem. Or, write like a moanhead if that makes you feel better. God knows how many moanhead entries I have!

There are many examples throughout Psalms where men of God cried out in pain and fear. For example, consider Psalm 10:1 that reads, "Why, LORD, do you stand far off? Why do you hide yourself in times of trouble?" Isn't it comforting to read the prayers of others who also felt alone, felt despair, and cried out to God through journaling? They wrote out their feelings, honestly, even though God had never left them.

Here is a wonderful example King David wrote during a time of despair. Psalm 13:

> "How long, LORD? Will you forget me forever? How long will you hide your face from me? How long must I wrestle with my thoughts and day after day have sorrow in my heart? How long will my enemy triumph over me? Look on me and answer, LORD my God. Give light to my eyes, or I will sleep in death, and my enemy will say, "I have overcome him," and my foes will rejoice when I fall. But I trust in your unfailing love; my heart rejoices in your salvation. I will sing the LORD's praise, for he has been good to me."

Notice David's attitude shift by the end, going back to his faith in God, going back to praising God despite the pain he clearly felt. When you write out your prayers, if you hear a response from God, write out His answer back to you as well. Write down any verses He uses to comfort you. Use your journal to keep track of all the ways God makes His presence known to you.

I have tons of entries that track what I call *God Winks*. Winks are the ways I feel God makes Himself tangibly known throughout the day. This includes the many times I've been out walking and I see a sign, a word, an object that God just spoke to me about or showed me in a dream. These moments are like when God sends you to a certain Scripture, then pays it off by having another person quote the same one. There are many ways God makes Himself known, presently and actively. I love keeping track of them because it builds my faith. (I later found out someone else also named these moments God Winks— SQuire Rushnell, who wrote a whole book series about them. He's become a good friend.)

Don't shy away from using creative writing. This isn't about talent and how well you can write. It's about your healing. It's about doing everything you can to express the emotions you may be stifling. Don't judge your writing as you're doing it. Just let the words flow honestly from your heart.

Remember: Our God is the greatest creative mind in the universe. Our resources, through Him, are endless.

CHAPTER 8
Travel Partners:
Telling Others

You gain strength, courage and confidence by every
experience in which you really stop to look fear in the face…
You must do the thing you cannot do.
(Eleanor Roosevelt)

Did you notice that I did not get any help until I started talking about my problem? If only I hadn't been so stubborn! It all started with telling a boyfriend. That relationship drove me into my first counseling session. Until I took that step, I made zero progress toward healing. I had to do it, no matter how hard it was or how embarrassing. Breaking the silence undercuts the power that panic has over us. Wouldn't you love to frustrate the power panic has over you?

Writing helped me get through the seasons when I was unable to speak. However, I had to stop hiding behind the page and climb way out of my comfort zone. Could I speak the words? Could I look someone in the face and admit my fears, pains, and hurts? I had little practice my whole life at being vulnerable and transparent. It's been a long journey for me to be able to open my mouth, learn to speak up, and finally let go of the idea that I have to project a perfect image to the world.

I finally joined the imperfect human race.

Are you ready to do that?

I couldn't just write about my experience anymore in the safety of my own bedroom. I had to reach out; I had to tell my story. I lived in the dark for too long. I didn't want anyone else to live where I did, especially when no one has to. I'm so thankful someone like Michael English came forward. If he hadn't, who knows how long it would have taken me to find out what was wrong with me!

I hope that in sharing my story, others will come to realize they're not alone. Do you still feel alone? Reach out to others with your story. You may find people who understand far more than you ever imagined!

It's time to break through your fear.

Break your silence.

A Step Forward

In the beginning, telling others was beyond hard. As you know, my first step was writing my screenplay, *Katie's Mountain*. When producers got interested in the project, I had to admit this story resonated with my own life. Resonated — that's the fancy way of admitting indirect connections. I had to be the example when we walked into network meetings. I gulped, "An example? You mean I have to tell someone I share my character's problem? I have to admit to television executives — who, incidentally, I've never met in my whole entire life — that Katie is like me? Are you nuts?" They weren't nuts; I just thought they were. But I did it! Yes, I, private, anxiety-ridden Cheryl, went to those meetings and admitted the truth. I truly wanted the movie to get made to help spread the message about how common anxiety disorders are. It's unfortunate that most anxiety depictions on television and in movies are side notes. Few depictions have called attention to this as a common mental challenge. I hope one day to change that.

Family Solace

I centered my script around three generations of women from the same family who have various forms of anxiety disorders. Once I started to talk about my struggles, I found others in my family who had the same problem. They had different triggers and fears, but I found out I wasn't alone. Panic often runs in families.

The first person outside my immediate family I told was my mother's sister, Jackie. My mother told me that she believed her sister struggled with anxiety when she was younger. I thought she might understand where I'm coming from.

As mentioned, I started with a letter. I did not tell her about the abuse at this point because I hadn't broken the silence with my parents. I didn't feel right about telling someone else in our family without having talked with my parents. So, I hid that part of the story. Here is an excerpt from a letter I wrote her:

> Jackie:
>
> I've battled a problem since I was twelve. I have an anxiety disorder. I've had many panic attacks, involuntarily, of course. My anxiety is directly related to guys. I have never been able to stay in relationships because I have panic attacks. I've never been able to let anyone get too close to me. Sometimes, I feel scared and wonder if I'll ever be able to get married. I want a husband and kids. But it's hard for me to see myself with someone, trusting him, and being okay. Where did I get my fears? I'm not sure. That's why I'm working so hard to figure that out. What I think it boils down to is that my number one fear is abandonment. I am so afraid to love someone because… what if it doesn't work out? What if I've got all these feelings for him and he leaves? I keep all emotions inside. Okay, so I'm working on that, too. I have to learn to let it out. Much of my life, I've spent putting on a happy face that says everything is fine. Internalizing

everything comes out in physical problems. But I'm also learning if I keep everyone away from me and protect myself with these anxiety attacks, then I will be missing out on one of the most wonderful things that can happen to a person. That's sharing life and love with someone else. That is why I am driven to work so hard, so I can eventually do just that. I am even going to write a book about my experience, in faith, that someday I will be better (so I can finish the book and write my final chapter, which I want my husband to co-author with me). I pray about it often. I believe I have issues to work through before I can get better. If God took it away without me doing the work, I'd be no better off. I would still be in the dark about what put me here and lose myself in a relationship trying too hard to be perfect.

My aunt was incredible. She wrote back with her story, showing her understanding and letting me know that I wasn't alone in my struggles. It touched me so much to know someone within my own family understood. While she didn't have the same fear of men, she still had similar issues, including a fear of abandonment. This came from having lost her father and grandmother both by the time she was five years old. Her mother (my grandmother) was left suddenly to raise five children on her own. Jackie was the youngest, so this took its toll on her the hardest. I'd like to share an excerpt of her letter back to me:

> *Cheryl:*
>
> *I lost my ability to trust. Like I couldn't trust that my mother would come back when she'd go out for the night! All that led to high anxiety whenever I got close to anyone. I've had many anxiety attacks over the years. I also spent years in therapy to help me to cope with them and understand them. The biggest thing seems to be identifying what brings them on and accepting that some of us are more susceptible for one*

reason or another, be it a genetic predisposition or environment, situation, or trauma. One of the tricky parts of the fears related to loss is that sometimes having that as the issue is an over-attachment to people and how we, in a sense, hand over our power to someone else to feel like we have an identity.

I was so amazed at the outpouring of love I received from my aunt. The letters exchanged were the beginning of an awesome bond. We knew each other's pain; we knew each other's fears. Finally, someone close to me understood. Not that I ever wanted anyone else to have this problem! After I came forward with this, anytime I was in Massachusetts, my aunt and I would get together so we could talk about progress.

Would I have known we had this in common if I'd never opened my mouth? No. I waited to confide in her about the abuse until after I had the chance to talk to my parents about it years later. But when I did open up, I received great empathy and understanding.

In 1997, my grandmother (Jackie's mother) got into a car accident. Physically, she only injured her knee, but emotionally, she became fearful. This accident triggered an anxiety disorder. She suddenly had trouble getting into cars and going out to eat in restaurants. She became borderline agoraphobic; she was only willing to leave the house to go to church, her usual bowling outings, or to a nursing home to visit one of her sisters. She could only handle what was part of her limited, normal routine. I used this as an opportunity to reach out to her and tell her about my struggles with panic.

Is there anyone in your family who has ever gone through this? Is there anyone you'd like to tell about your experience? Perhaps you can help one who is dealing with similar challenges.

A Caravan of Friends
I didn't stop with telling my family; I learned how to talk to friends as

well. I walked the road that I no longer traveled alone; I had others beside me. Even the friends who didn't share anything like my problem were certainly there for me to lean on.

Openness and honesty changes relationships; it strengthens them. There is virtually nothing to lose by sharing, but everything to gain.

There is the rare occasion someone will not be able to handle your pain. Don't let that stop you from taking the risk of being open. My friendships and relationships since then have grown much stronger.

I came forward with my story, for the first time in a group, in 2004 at a women's prayer group. It touched me to see everyone related to me on different levels. We understand fear. Unfortunately, too many understand abuse. I was nervous about sharing but was glad I did. The week before I decided to share, two women in our group were discussing that they'd had panic attacks recently. They wondered if anyone else in the room could relate, stating that no one ever talks about this problem. Their honesty helped give me the courage to tell my whole story. Their honesty reminded me of how people who experience panic attacks feel alone because of everyone's silence.

In Search of Like-Minded Lambs
Another way to talk to others with similar struggles is to join support groups, either locally or online. Check with local churches to see if they have a group. Go online to find chat rooms and message boards. I spent time reading posts online. You can post anonymously if that will help you get started in being open.

A Voyage in Bravery
Once I found out that my problem had a traceable cause, I decided to go back to Nathan and tell him about my past. It was three months after we'd broken up. I hadn't been able to go near him since, without having anxiety attacks. I knew, no matter how humiliated the physical symptoms would make me feel, I had to go through with it. Once I knew my problem had a cause, I wanted to go back and explain myself.

The day I chose to tell Nathan my story, I had anxiety attacks for hours. My body was exhausted from throwing up over and over. I did what I could to control the circumstances of where we'd meet and when. I, for once, put my own needs above how I may have looked. I didn't even try to put up the appearance of being anxiety-free.

When he tried to suggest we meet for a short while and then see a movie, I said no. I wanted his time, and I needed to control the environment. I chose a botanical garden where I knew I could enjoy God's creation, peace, and outdoor air. I didn't let any of his innocent suggestions sway me from what I needed. When I first saw him that day, I laid out the warning—that I would most likely get sick. That's just the way it was and I wasn't going to fight it. It was still embarrassing when I had to leave him for a few moments to throw up, but I chose not to care. The idea that I was about to tell the truth about the abuse for the first time ever to a man was frightening. Anyone would struggle with that. I didn't have to condemn myself for it.

We sat among the beautiful flower gardens on a private bench. Then I recounted my story—the story that helped me finally understand myself. I cried through it. (You know, that other thing I never did in public!) I didn't care; it felt necessary. For the first time ever, I gave myself permission to be imperfect and vulnerable with a guy.

While there was no chance of rekindling that particular relationship, it was important to me that he understand I wasn't a freak for no reason. I was still feeling like a freak, even if I was beginning to understand why. He was supportive and gentle.

I wish I could say talking to him honestly about my problem helped me hang around him without anxiety. The talk happened in May 1996. It wasn't until August that I was able to be around him, comfortably, without panic attacks. I still got sick whenever he would visit, even though we were just friends. I was so used to associating this man with panicking that just the thought of seeing him brought on fear. It's the *fear of fear* reaction, when we convince ourselves that because we panicked in the past, we'll panic again. It took me from the breakup in February until August to grow out of this reaction. Thankfully, it's allowed us to keep our friendship that remains strong today. I am thankful I didn't run from him, despite my embarrassment.

A Meander Backwards

Despite these small steps toward personal openness, I feared getting back into relationships and chose to stay away from them. Imagine my struggle. It's important to be open about the disorder, to remove its teeth. But how do you open up to a person the moment you start dating? Before someone gets to know you well, it hardly seems appropriate to share such personal details. I didn't know how to overcome this extreme challenge. My solution was a bad one. After my relationship with Nathan, I stayed away from dating for five and a half years. I didn't have the guts to dive back in. I may have understood myself better, but I was far from healed of my anxiety disorder.

I spent the next five years trying not to think about dating and stayed busy with my writing and planning life changes. I told others those changes were in the way of me even looking for a relationship. I always knew I wanted to move to California. I spent a few years saving up for that big change. I told everyone I didn't want to date in North Carolina because I'd eventually be moving; I didn't want anyone holding me back. When my sister suggested I date a guy in the singles class at church, I said no. (Plus, he wasn't asking me out!)

In 2000, I made it to California. I busied myself with getting used to my new home, making new friends, and writing books and tapes with Frank Peretti. I also had to keep up with a full-time job at a TV network. My busy schedule kept me from having to think about relationships. Again, it became my defense, my excuse.

A New Safari

About a year and half after I moved to California, I woke up to the fact that if I didn't give myself permission to try again — and possibly fail — I would never get married. I was twenty-nine years old. It was time to test and see if any of the therapy in 1996 paid off.

In Summer 2001, a friend of mine who's gifted in the Holy Spirit with words of prophecy told me that I would be going on a trip where I'd meet someone. I knew which trip this was; it was already planned. Yet she didn't know I was going on one. That's how I knew it was God speaking. God prepared me on purpose.

Left to my own devices, I'm likely to ignore any male possibilities that could be smack in front of me. His divine preparation alerted me to keep my eyes open.

My eyes landed right on one guy in particular.

I'll call him Richard. He was adorable. He found me adorable as well. I knew Richard was the one God spoke about. Richard and I spent hours talking this particular weekend. We clicked right away; mutual attraction was there! I was nervous, but thankfully, I did not have any panic attacks. It was the normal, first-date butterflies. In fact, it was fun. I repeatedly told myself that just because I felt those butterflies did not mean I would panic.

After that weekend, Richard and I started dating. Because he was unusually open with personal details about his own struggles, it made it easier for me to be transparent. On our third date, I revealed my heart. I told him about my panic disorder, my problems with guys, and the abuse. It was an incredibly vulnerable thing for me to do, but I knew I needed to be honest. I needed to see how he'd react to my potential problem while also relieving the pressure of hiding my story.

He reacted wonderfully. He even tried to find ways to equate his own anxieties in life with mine, even if they didn't exactly apply. (It was completely adorable of him to try!) He found my problem a little endearing. It didn't take long for all nerves to subside. For the first time, I made it through a relationship without a single panic attack.

Richard and I hit a point in the relationship where we sensed we weren't compatible long-term. I wanted the relationship to work, yet, I felt like there was a high possibility that it was not the right one for either of us. It was my first normal breakup, having nothing to do with anxiety.

When I sensed it was going to end, I worked it out on paper:

> *Cheryl's Journal (September 30, 2001)*
>
> *As one who normally guards her heart, I've allowed myself to hope. But tonight, I lie awake, afraid to allow myself much hope. I will be disappointed if this relationship doesn't work out. But I also feel like I'm still guarded. Like part of me doesn't want to give up that emotional control that would allow me to fall in love. I feel like I'm still in self-preservation mode.*

Because Richard and I mutually decided it was not going to work, I'm thankful I was guarded. However, it was a defense I was going to have to break down so I could finally fall in love with someone. It saddened me when this groundbreaking relationship ended, but I left it knowing much good had come out of it. Right after the breakup, I was able to see this:

> *Cheryl's Journal (October 02, 2001)*
>
> *I need to look at this as a good thing. I got practice at having a relationship, learning to communicate, and expressing myself. I will mourn this loss. I hate that I have to start over. But Lord, there's no denying you had purpose in this relationship. You even told me about it before it happened. Once the pain subsides, I'll be thankful I had this experience. I will grow and move on from this.*

Perhaps that person was brought into my life as a chance to safely practice dating. I learned a lot about how to be open with a man. It was a great experience. It made me hunger to find *the one* who was right for me.

One month later, I started dating someone new; I'll save that story for Chapter 11.

Traveling Lambs

I hope the message of this chapter sinks in. Take the time to tell other people. Speak honestly about who you are, faults and all. It can bring great healing to you.

If you are having a tough time explaining your struggles with someone you love, try writing it out. Share some of the writing you did for the Chapter 7 assignments. Or give them a book to read — like this one — that explains where you are coming from. Highlight pieces that speak to your personal situation.

If you are reading this book as one who does not suffer — but, rather, as one who wants to know more about this disorder and how to help someone you know — I offer this advice. Be willing to draw them out. This is an embarrassing problem for anyone who has it. It's hard to open up. Ask questions about it. Make it easy on the one who is trying to bear these truths that make them blush. Give them a safe place to share their struggles.

It's hard for me to imagine there was a time I didn't speak my mind, a time when I felt like I had to conform to what someone else wanted so I'd be liked and accepted. Truthfully, those who love me do so for who I am, not how I conform to what I think they want.

I have grown so much since I first stepped into that counselor's office in 1996. I believe this growth happened through a mixture of God's help, soul-searching, prayer, and being honest with myself and others about my problem. Learning to communicate and accept myself the way I am — faults and all — has made a huge difference in how I see myself in this world.

I used to say that I never wanted to tell people the truth because I was afraid I'd lose them. Instead, I learned to face relationships with a new boldness, a confidence that I never had before. I got over hiding behind protective walls out of fear of losing people.

Now, I'm free.

I'm free to be me — warts and all. Honesty is way better than keeping everything bottled up inside. If we do that, our bodies will rebel against all that stress. So, why bother trying to hide?

Beyond the Comfort Zone

This brings me to the topic of writing this book. For years since counseling, I'd been gathering all sorts of journal writings. I thought one day, they may form a book that could help people, but I was always afraid of the idea. Until this point, I had control over who did or didn't know about my problems. Writing a book changes that. I started to chicken out of the idea of doing this.

Then one day, I was praying to God about it. I felt like He was prompting me to work on telling my story. I said, "Are you sure, Lord? Do I have to?" He replied, "Yes, I'm sure." I smiled sheepishly, saying, "Are you really, really sure? Positively? I mean, I don't mind abandoning the project, forgetting the whole thing and just keeping my little mouth shut."

God had other ideas — another plan that was not my own. It would be so easy to hide, so easy to stay silent, but my drive to reach out to others won out. I wanted to use this book to break the embarrassment cycle.

Do you have a story to tell? Is there a book you should write? Is there a group you should lead at your church or community center, using a book like this one? Is there a public speaking engagement you should consider? Perhaps you can reach out to others as well.

God likes to nudge us out of our comfort zones. For those of us with panic problems, that is not a place we want to be. Ever. We'd rather be safe, cozy, in control, and as far away from discomfort as possible.

God continues to remind me that my life is not about comfort or an easy road. My life is in His hands for Him to use as He pleases. Does that mean forcing myself into situations that make me uncomfortable?

According to Him, it sometimes does. So, there! God made me do this. I take great comfort in the fact that if anyone is helped through this, it can redeem the challenging and painful experiences.

For all of us, personal openness should be one of our biggest goals toward battling anxiety.

Stop hiding.

Come out and join the rest of the imperfect human race.

Now it's time to journey toward peace.

PART III

The Peace

CHAPTER 9

Paving the Way:
Roads Toward Peace

I have learned this at least by my experiment: that if one
advances confidently in the direction of his dreams, and
endeavors to live the life which he has imagined, he
will meet with a success unexpected in common hours.
(Henry David Thoreau)

Did you know there are so many productive tasks you can do to help
yourself through anxiety attacks? Did you know there are plenty of
ways to let God help you?

This chapter covers many coping methods. You don't need all of
them. I'm just giving you an overview of the many I experimented with
that helped me through. Try them all to see which ones help you. I
went to a support group one night and everyone shouted out their
favorite anxiety coping techniques. To follow is a sampling of that list:

Breathing Exercises
Relaxation
Self-Talk/Positive Thinking
Visualization
Humor
Distractions
Prayer

Exercise

Meditation

Therapy

Massage

Scripture

Aroma Therapy

Medication

Reading

Television/Movies

Music

Desensitization

I will discuss the coping techniques which helped me throughout this chapter: relaxation exercises, visualization, desensitization, setting goals, medication, using note cards, and letting God help through prayer, dreams, visions, and dialoguing with Him.

The more you can give yourself to do during an attack, the more active you'll be. It puts you in the driver's seat instead of allowing yourself to become a passive victim to anxiety. If you learn good coping techniques during peaceful moments, you'll already know what to do when you are about to have a panic attack.

Start by asking yourself the right questions during an attack:

What am I doing that could be contributing to this panic?

What can I do to help myself now?

Perhaps some of the following techniques can be used to help you through anxious times:

Relaxation Exercises
These are relaxation exercises my counselor suggested I do.

TENSE / RELEASE EXERCISE:

Lie down on the floor. Tense your body for ten seconds then relax your body for the next ten. Try it several times. Then write in your journal how your body feels during both states. Be descriptive. Did you notice if you held your breath while you were tense? Repeat the exercise again. This time, afterwards, get up and walk around. Do you feel calmer than before you started the exercise? This exercise is intended to get you used to focusing on your body during a time of tension and relaxation, so you can recognize both states. Did the moment you were tense start to make you feel anxious? If so, your body is associating those tensions with an anxiety attack.

BREATHING EXERCISE:

Lie on the floor. Practice breathing from your diaphragm. Take ten seconds to inhale, another ten to exhale. Pay attention to how your lower abdomen moves up and down. Concentrate on breathing deep, cleansing breaths. Do this ten times lying on your back on the floor, feeling your stomach's movements. Then, do it ten times while standing or walking around. This can help you get used to deep, cleansing breaths while active, a skill that is important during an attack.

Sometimes, breathing properly can slow symptoms down, even if they don't stop completely. If you do feel symptoms coming on, take a quick inventory of how you're breathing. Is your breathing pattern too fast or too shallow?

If you do the exercise, you'll start to memorize how it feels to take deep breaths. You'll know right away if you're not breathing deeply enough. If you feel panic coming on, let your mind focus on breathing; it gives you something active to do. Breathing is an important ally during a panic attack. We have to get (or keep) control of it. It can help or hurt us, depending on how we use it. If you breathe too rapidly or shallowly, you'll make yourself even more anxious. You could bring on hyperventilation.

Visualization / Imagination

What's going on in our minds during an attack is very important. I will discuss at length in Chapter 10 the words streaming through our minds. The way we think is so important, I've devoted an entire chapter to that technique alone. I'll teach you how to rewrite the lies we feed ourselves.

Here, I will discuss the pictures in our minds. We need to make sure we are not visualizing our failure or catastrophic events. Have you ever noticed how just imagining something terrible can elicit a physical and emotional response? Our imaginations are very powerful. Why not use them as our allies?

If you have a tendency to imagine the worst, you must break that habit! Easier said than done, right? How do we stop our minds from picturing bad things? Well, you can start by replacing the bad picture with a good one.

You need to give your imagination something else to see. You can't just stop the bad picture and expect it not to plop right back down in front of your mind's eye. You need to paint a new, positive picture. Paint a picture that can speak to your heart. Pictures are a language of the heart. That's why we feel our emotions stir when using visualization.

Think of the exercise where I suggested you write a scene that depicts you (or your fictional character) not having a panic attack in a situation where you previously did. You can do the same thing with your imagination. Visualize yourself being successful in your mind. Use your imagination to walk yourself through a possible panic situation—then, watch yourself responding and acting normally.

Hey, you can even go for confidence! This can be just as effective as acting out the scene in a mirror. You can remember this scene as it played out in your imagination the next time you find yourself in a panic situation. Ponder this image. Let it help you walk through the scene in real life the way you imagined it.

As we will explore in great depth in Chapter 10, it's important what our minds tell us. We need to speak positive words and feed positive pictures to our minds. This is one way to do that. If we ponder thoughts and images of ourselves failing, we will have a tough time stopping those from becoming a self-fulfilling prophecy.

I would like to offer one caution about using your imagination. Be careful not to daydream about the life you wish you had more than you participate in the real world. Many times throughout my life, I got too caught up in daydreams. I found myself so disappointed when life never lived up to them. (Annoyingly, life never did!) I think this degree of fantasizing can slow down the healing process, especially if there are hurts we need to get over.

For example, have you ever suffered a bad breakup? Did you spend time fantasizing about the hundreds of ways this person came back to apologize, declare he was wrong, and how he wants you back? Nothing slows down getting over a lost love more! I urge you to use your imagination for healing purposes only, not fantasizing about all that will most likely never happen. That will just lead to disappointments and disillusionment with life. And who needs that?

Let's put healing visualization into practice.

VISUALIZATION ASSIGNMENT #1:

Take a situation that brings on anxiety. (For example, a trip in a car, an elevator, a date, a grocery store line, or sitting in a restaurant.) Imagine yourself facing that fear without having a panic attack. Watch yourself go through the motions without fear. Write down in your journal how this makes you feel. Write down what you did in your imagination; emotionally capture your success.

VISUALIZATION ASSIGNMENT #2:

Come up with a list of at least five of your favorite Bible verses that encourage peace. Memorize them. Come up with a visual picture for the verse. You can bring this image to memory during an attack. It will help pull you into a right-brain, heart function. It works better than only reciting the words of the verse. Here are some examples:

Verse: Psalm 94:19: "When anxiety was great within me, your consolation brought me joy."

Picture: Imagine yourself on a peaceful hillside, sitting on the grass next to Jesus, His arm around you as you say these words to Him. Imagine His smile, His kind eyes.

Verse: Philippians 4:6: "Do not be anxious about anything, but in every situation, by prayer and petition, with thanksgiving, present your requests to God."

Picture: Imagine yourself handing something that represents your problem over to Jesus. Imagine kneeling at His feet while He speaks words of peace to you. (This can turn into a session of dialoguing with Jesus. Write down any of the calming words you feel He speaks to you.)

Verse: 1 Peter 5:7: "Cast all your anxiety on him because he cares for you."

Picture: Imagine Jesus taking a large bag full of things that represent your problems on His back and walking beside you.

Verse: Psalm 23:4 (kjv): "Yea, though I walk through the valley of the shadow of death, I will fear no evil: for thou art with me; thy rod and thy staff they comfort me."

Picture: Choose your own version of the "valley of the shadow of death." Choose a picture of the situation that causes you to panic. Then, replay the "dangerous" scene, visualizing Jesus by your side, walking through it with you, there to protect you.

I once imagined myself as a lamb walking between two mountains down in the rocky valley on a day where the sun cast many shadows. My shadow, instead of looking like the body of a lamb, looked like the shape of Jesus in a robe, right behind me.

VISUALIZATION ASSIGNMENT #3:

"Create your safe place"

Create in your mind a place you feel is safe. This can be real or imaginary. It can be pieces of many different places you've been where you felt peaceful. There aren't any rules. Let it be a place you can retreat to — in your mind — when you're experiencing anxiety. You could use an actual photograph if you have one. (We have original, black and white photographs printed on the pages of the *Finally Fearless Workbook*.) Postcards from resort towns are a great source of God's beauty. You can paint your own picture in your mind. Or, if you're an artist, you may want to sketch or paint this place as well.

To follow is the journal entry I wrote for my counselor about my safe place:

> *My safe place is called "Winds of Summer." It's a cottage that rests above the shore to the beach. It has a porch with a white porch swing. It's always a cool summer night at this special place with a light, healing breeze blowing as it ripples the water and washes over my soul. The only sound: waves cascading over the shore. The moon and stars shine brightly and reflect on the water. What is this place? It's the safe haven where I escape when I can't handle the stress, the place where I visualize myself sitting when I get anxious. It's a place where I feel free with my emotions. It's okay to cry here. I'm alone. It's almost a joy to cry because tears can flow freely without hiding or anyone asking, "What's wrong?" It's a release. I also can sing a praise song to God here. There's something about being close to nature that draws me into God and His peace. No one eavesdrops here. It's just God and me, the wind and the waves. I can imagine my anxieties whisked up by the wind and taken up toward God; He can handle those anxieties much better than I can. It's the type of place, that if I weren't alone in it, my friends and I would be*

discussing deep issues. We'd play Truth or Dare. We'd dig deep into the heart and soul of each of us. There's openness here. So, whenever I start to feel the impending doom, I try to picture myself on my porch swing, breathing the fresh saltwater air. Those winds are the most cleansing and healing winds that wash over me.

Desensitization

Desensitization is an important coping technique; it's the way you practice facing your fears. For example, if you are afraid to eat in restaurants, set smaller goals to work up to face that fear. Start with your imagination, visualizing your success in a restaurant. Then, try eating on the patio of a restaurant where you'll have more air. Next time, try to eat at a table inside. Then, work your way up to sitting on the outside of a booth, then inside. Give yourself permission to grow in stages.

Wanting to use desensitization was frustrating for me. How was I supposed to practice? I couldn't just date if no one was asking or if I wasn't interested. Plus, just dating any random *Joe* for practice would not have done me any good. I had to like the person for my irrational fears to kick up. (Yeah, how convenient. I'd be fine if I *didn't* like the guy. What fun is that?) Finding someone to fall deeply in love with was not something I could control. Hopefully, you have a situation where you can get practice before you have to face your fears.

Set Goals

Make a list of goals you want to accomplish to battle your anxiety disorder: progress you'd like to make, actions you'd like to take without anxiety. Think of small steps first, then, set larger goals. Be proactive instead of waiting for something to change.

My list started with counseling. Then I wanted to redeem locations, like restaurants, so I could enjoy them again. I needed to feel safe again in public, around other people in normal social settings. I did all of these in steps. I needed to get the rest of my world back up to its normal size before I felt comfortable adding dating to the mix.

Medication

I will not cover medication in-depth here. I will just share what my experience was with anti-anxiety pills, when I chose to use them and when I didn't. The answer to the question of whether or not to use them is going to be different for everyone. I can't speak to your particular situation like a medical doctor can. What I will offer is a personal testimony on how I used them.

For a long time, I refused to even consider using anything. I was so afraid I would get addicted. As you probably know, we can get dependent on some anti-anxiety medications. I took refusing them to the extreme. There were times I suffered unnecessarily because I was so against taking them.

My counselor suggested I get a prescription for a fast-acting drug to keep on hand in case of emergencies. Considering I didn't have panic every single day of my life, I didn't need a prescription drug every day. I finally went to a doctor, asking for this little piece of emergency relief. I used it as a backup. I was always glad to know I had it as my extra security cushion even though I tried not to use it.

I also learned, during the process of desensitization (that is, once I finally did have someone I could practice dating with), it helped for me to use medication at the beginning of a relationship.

I usually told myself that I didn't need it; I was only taking it as a backup to boost my confidence. I'd take it before a first, second, and third date with a guy, just to have some experiences where I could be with the person and not have much anxiety. This helped me see myself in a dating situation without panic. It built my confidence. I also fed myself the belief that I would have been fine without it. By the fourth or fifth date, I would try a date without taking it. I'd have it with me in case I needed it.

To follow is a journal entry, when I first started dating Richard:

Cheryl's Journal (July 2001)

At first, I decided to be kind to myself. I allowed myself to take one pill before the first date. I figured I needed the extra confidence. I wasn't sure if I needed it, but I didn't want to find out too late that I did. I was perfectly calm for most of the day. This is a real victory.

On the third date, when I told Richard my personal story, he was surprised I had any problems with fear. He said he saw no signs of it in me. That's when I admitted I'd been taking pills to help me. He told me he was cool with that, but if I ever wanted to try a date without one, he'd welcome it—even if it meant I wouldn't be okay. He wanted me to know it was safe to try. I did try on our next two dates without telling him. For our sixth date, he asked if I wanted to give this experiment a try. Imagine his joy when I told him I'd already done it! I warned him that it didn't mean I would never need them. I wanted to give myself the permission to use them if I ever had to. Thankfully, I never needed pills again in that relationship.

I think it was right of me to give myself permission to use that crutch on the first couple of dates. There is nothing wrong with that; it wasn't a failure. It helped me be around a cute guy without having an anxiety attack. It gave me an inventory of successes to draw from so I could eventually stop using the crutch. When I stopped taking it, I convinced myself I never needed it to begin with. True or not, it worked!

A month after that relationship ended, I started dating someone new. Again, I started out with one pill before the first couple of dates. Once my confidence was built, I backed off. Had I demanded perfection, I wouldn't have allowed myself that comfort of pills. I could have worked myself into a full-blown attack and relearned being afraid of men and dating relationships. It could have been disastrous. Instead, I said "Okay, Cheryl, you're allowed to do something nice for yourself to make it through the beginning awkwardness." And again, I was happy with the results.

Have you talked to your doctor or counselor about what's best for you, regarding medication? Let them help you decide.

Note Cards

Keep little note cards in your purse, book bag, or back pocket that remind you of your coping techniques when you're too frazzled to think straight. My cards ranged from breathing techniques to descriptions of visual pictures to peaceful Bible promises. Sometimes, I'd just stare at them, unable to concentrate or absorb their words. But other times, the meaning of the words broke through, and I was able to use their contents to pull myself back from the anxious feelings.

I shared all the previous techniques because they were helpful to me. But guess what? None of them, in and of themselves, are the answer; none of them healed me. That's why they're called coping techniques; they help you deal with panic while you are still battling your disorder. But what about a true healing?

I believe the only way to heal is through God and His counsel.

God as Our Counselor

As I've emphasized throughout this book, anxiety disorders indicate that our hearts need healing. Therefore, we need to march this problem straight to God, the Healer of our hearts. Many of us need our self-image restored as well. All the calm breaths in the world can't do that. They may relieve symptoms, so these exercises are important to know. We need to let God counsel us and clean up our hearts.

Malcolm Smith in *Freedom From Fear* says, "Many believers are trapped in their anxieties because they have never thought through the implications of what they believe. If God is with us, then there is no place for worry and anxiety. Freedom from worry, fretting, and anxiety is not a miracle in our emotions, but is a result of the conclusions of a Holy Spirit-enlightened mind. God's command to change our anxious behavior is based on the reality of His presence." (1)

We need to allow God to take on the role of Counselor in our lives. As you can tell from my twenty-year journey, I didn't make much progress for a long time. I believe it's because I didn't know how to hear God. I knew how to pray and cry out, but I always believed He just wasn't listening. And if He was, I felt He wasn't responding.

No one ever taught me what I needed to know to hear and recognize God's voice. And it's not the intention of this book to teach you exactly how to do that, as many other authors have tackled that topic such as Mark and Patti Virkler in their book, *Dialogue With God*. What I learned from that book changed my life and revolutionized my relationship with God. Their ministry, Communion With God, can supply you with books and tapes on this subject. (You can also download free information about this from their website, www.cwgministries.org.)

Here, I will share with you some examples of the ways God has spoken to me. Much of this was toward the end of my panic journey. I wish I had known how to hear Him sooner. I probably would have healed a lot quicker. Maybe you already know how to converse with God. If so, that's wonderful! Let Him counsel you about your fears.

I will give you examples of several ways God has counseled me: through His still small voice, through journaling, and through dreams and visions.

To follow are samples of words God spoke to me when I asked Him to speak to my heart about where I was emotionally at the time:

> (June 2003)
>
> God: *Rejoice in Me, again I say rejoice. A time of healing is here. Hear My calling. You are My child, My beauty, My Ruby. Trust in Me, for I am trustworthy. I'm the*

Rock of your salvation. You are Mine. You are in the palm of My hand. I won't let go. Rest in Me. Put Me first; keep Me first. I am a jealous God. You are precious in My sight. Trust. Walk the paths I set before you. I meet you where you are. I heal, I mend, I shape, I reveal in My timing. I am sovereign, a ruler. You can trust Me. I am the "I Am." Everlasting. I do speak. Listen. Others walk away. I don't walk away. Depend on Me. My love is sufficient. Nothing else matters but Me.

(November 2003)

God: My waters are healing as you walk hand in hand with Me by peaceful waters. It is a time, a time to enjoy a peace you've never known. I am with you. I always was, in the midst of it all. I think you know that now; you feel it now. You've submitted your will and heart. I make hearts whole. Remember the peace I offer is unmatched by any substance, anything that numbs or forces you to forget. Your whole life has been a journey you haven't walked alone. Your anxieties are finally cast on Me. Your healing can help other people. You can teach and help from a place that knows pain. I will flow through you, My child.

(December 2003)

God: Our relationship needs communion so I can deal with you directly where you are. I know where you are at all times, both physically and emotionally. I can speak to your spirit truths that you can use to handle situations. Listen for Me, especially when you don't know what to do. Remember Me before you react. Listen for Me. My leading is there for the taking. I can illuminate My Scriptures to you in a way that is meaningful to your life. Those words do not pass away; their meanings are still true today and can be applied.

Those who lived during the writing of My Word lived through similar struggles and pains you experience. I can use them to teach you. Many times you read and wonder why they weren't smarter, why they stayed in the wilderness so long, yet in your own experience you choose to be in the same place. So, you understand their journey. They are not as foreign as they may seem. Think of the complainers in Moses's time who were never satisfied. Once they got what they thought they wanted, again, they grew tired of it and complained for something else. This is something you can relate to. No one is ever satisfied, and they won't be until My return. You are incomplete, and you will be until that time, when I, the Author and Perfecter of your faith, return to complete the good work I started. Make Me your joy. My joy is everlasting. This world's joy is temporary.

Those are just a few examples of the healing words God has spoken to my heart. I will show you more examples in Chapter 11, as well as in the Appendix where I will share my journal entries from one of the most difficult seasons of my life. It contains both my outcries to God as well as His answers back.

Dream Interpretation

Do you believe your dreams are just products of what you ate the night before? If so, you could be missing some of God's most pertinent messages. There are several books available on dreams and how God still uses them today. (See the bibliography for a list.) I encourage you to read books by Christian authors who base their research on biblical principles. Don't resist this method of God's counsel. God spoke through dreams so many times in the Bible. What makes us think He's changed today? Why have so many of us closed the door on God and chosen not to listen?

As it reads in Acts 2:17 (kjv), "And it shall come to pass in the last days, saith God, I will pour out of my Spirit upon all flesh: and your sons and your daughters shall prophesy, and your young men shall see visions, and your old men shall dream dreams."

Daniel, in the Old Testament, says the reason you dream is so you can "know the thoughts of thy heart" (Daniel 2:30, kjv).

Psalm 16:7 says, "I will praise the Lord, who counsels me; even at night my heart instructs me."

Notice that two of these verses talk about the heart. What's going on in your heart? Your dreams can show you.

One of the classes I took through Christian Leadership University was *Wisdom Through Dream Interpretation*. I believe it's important both to study how this works as well as to leave our minds open to the Holy Spirit's leading. I do not recommend getting a dictionary of symbols to figure out what your dreams mean. Usually, symbols in your dreams are as personal to you as your life experiences. No book can assign a meaning to the symbols. (This is also why should not depend solely on other people to interpret your dreams.)

In Herman Riffel's book *Dream Interpretation: A Biblical Understanding*, he says, "The basic purpose of a dream is to show us the thoughts of our hearts over…the thoughts of our mind. All day long we operate by the thoughts of our mind, with its reasoning and deliberations. When the mind is still, God speaks to our innermost being through the thoughts of our heart in the dream…. God's ultimate purpose for our dreams is to bring us to wholeness." (2)

Just like when we talk with God in prayer and He replies in His still small voice, God can speak direction, exhortation, encouragement, or a solution to a problem we're facing through dreams.

God got my attention in the way He uses dreams when He sent me eight prophetic dreams about the same upcoming event. I didn't know at the time that's what He was doing. But once I saw the events unfold in reality, I realized that God had spoken. I will tell you that story in Chapter 11. Those dreams were the catalyst for me to go out and research dreams and God's use of them. Since then, I've been receiving the most amazing dreams from God. Once I was open to it and started listening, God sent many counseling dreams. (They will be captured in a future book.)

Dreams can paint an accurate picture of where we are emotionally. God has frequently showed me the condition of my heart through dreams. He's helped me see where I am on my journey toward healing through them. This is my favorite way God has spoken because the visions He's shown me are forever with me. The pictures are so vivid that I could not have made them up on my own. I am now a sponge ready to soak up whatever God would like to show me through dreams.

In the same way that we can feel frightened during a dream, we can experience joy and healing. Have you ever noticed how real dreams seem? Have you ever been angry with someone for what they did to you in a dream — yet it was only a dream? Have you ever had an awesome dream and noticed a lift in your mood? Dreams are powerful in stirring emotions.

The first step in receiving dreams from God, so they can be useful to us, is to record them right after we have them. Then ask God for interpretations.

In general, I believe we need to learn to hear from God ourselves, then check what we hear with the mentors and counselors who know us. I don't think we should become overly dependent upon looking to others to tell us what our dreams mean, especially those we have no relationship with personally. Let God build relationship with you when He sends you a dream, rather than trying to depend on someone else's relationship with God by asking them to figure out God's message for you. Just make sure the interpretation is coming to you, by way of the Holy Spirit, not something you are forcing. God may not give you insight immediately. But do know this: whatever He tells you will not violate Scripture or tell you to do something contrary to what He's already advised in His Word. Once you go through this process, then you can check your dream and its interpretation with a trusted mentor or spiritual counselor to see if they bear witness to what you're sensing. Again, this should preferably be someone who knows you. (You can do the same with anything you write down in your personal dialoguing with God.)

By the time God started speaking through dreams, I already knew how to hear His voice in dialoguing. One night, I was praying about God's use of dreams and this was His response:

> *Cheryl's Journal (2003)*
>
> *God: Start writing down whatever you remember from your dreams. I will reveal things to you. As you write them down, you'll remember more details. Expect Me to speak and reveal the condition of your heart or truths about others. You can be used this way. You're already visual; you can be more. Trust Me to take over. You will get caught up in My Spirit. I will send you dreams of wise counsel, dreams that direct you, heal you. I love that you want to hear from Me this way. I am a creative God, and I love to paint pictures. Keep listening to those pictures. Look at them, meditate on them. Ask Me for My interpretation of them. I am there for you. I will speak to you. I will lead you. Walk with Me daily; you are My child who walks with Me.*

I was excited about this! I started writing down my dreams and asking God to interpret them. And He did! I had a blast with this, even when I didn't like His direction for me. After I'd been hearing from God through this method for almost a year, God chose a very creative way to confirm for me that it was truly His voice. During a season when I'd received lots of dreams, I told God that if He woke me up in the middle of the night, I'd be faithful and record the dream into my tape recorder. (We remember our dreams much better if we awaken right after having them, rather than trying to remember them all in the morning.)

One night, He woke me up at 3:00 a.m. I recorded the dream. Before going back to sleep, I muttered, "God, if You want to send me another dream tonight, wake me up again and I'll record it." Around 5:00 a.m., the Lord woke me up again. I was rather tired by this point. And this time, I felt the dream seemed too silly to bother writing down. I said, "Lord, that dream must not mean anything. I'm going back to sleep."

I slept a mere minute, long enough to dream of a fly buzzing around my head. The noise woke me up, but of course, there was no actual fly in my room. I pondered the previous dream again and said, "God, that dream still seems silly to me. I'm not recording it." Again, I drifted back to sleep.

So, what did God do? Again, the buzzing started. Talk about God's alarm clock! I woke up to its loudness and was like, "Fine! You must want me to record this." I lazily muttered the dream into my recorder. I don't necessarily feel that dream was of major importance. I think God was insisting I obey what I told Him I'd do.

Now, here's where God's sense of humor shines! About a month later, I read Benny Thomas's book, *Exploring the World of Dreams.* It was a textbook for my class. While it was in my possession for months, I hadn't looked at it yet. One night, I sat down to read this book and couldn't put it down. Suddenly, I landed on a page where Mr. Thomas relayed a most curious story: one night, God woke him up using the sound of a fly buzzing around his head in a dream.

When I read that, I could not stop laughing. I was in awe of the amazing way God chose to confirm the validity of the dreams He'd been giving me! What a creative and cute way He did it! God knew I would eventually read this account and recognize it!

Isn't God just so awesome? I hope you'll open your heart to this. While I always knew God was speaking, the way He confirmed it for me was delightful.

To illustrate how dreams can help us, I will give you two examples where God counseled me toward emotional health during a season of depression in 2004.

DREAM ONE:

I went to bed one night, depressed. I welcomed God to send me a message through a dream, again telling Him He could wake me up in the middle of the night so I would know the dream was important. (He likes waking me up at 3:00.) In the dream, I went on a date with a friend's boyfriend. I felt horribly guilty. I knew what I was doing would hurt this friend. The guy and I ended up in the backseat of his car, kissing. In my real life at the time, I was in much pain over a breakup. In the dream, I recalled this same pain. I knew I was only cheating with this guy to try to feel better for one night. I was excusing my hurtful actions. Yet, I wasn't sure how I was going to face my friend.

Interpretation:

When I first woke up from this dream, I immediately thought the dream meant nothing. There was no way I'd cheat with a friend's boyfriend. That's just not me! But later that morning, I felt prompted to ask the question, "Where in my life am I being unfaithful?" If you read more about dream interpretation, you'll see that looking at what's happening in the dream — the main action — can help you figure out how it applies to your life. In the dream, I was being unfaithful to a friend. In my life, I was being unfaithful to God. I had a close, yet volatile, relationship with God then. I was using sinful means to try to cover up my pain (the same pain I had in the dream). I knew God was trying to counsel me by showing me the condition of my heart through this dream. I'd been giving myself permission to do things that I shouldn't do, just to slap a temporary bandage on my pain.

After I realized this dream was about my relationship with God, I welcomed Him to speak to me further. I believe He answered me with the following:

"Drink from My waters. They are living. Everything else is deadly or wrought with poisons. Your well does not need to be dry. Call upon Me for fresh, living waters. Press in to Me. Do not push Me away. Do not numb or anesthetize yourself. It will not last. Those roads lead to death and destruction.

Where you look are dead-ends. They will not fulfill you. Your anger with Me thwarts your growth and plans. Stop running. This is your time to refuel, to lean on Me for your divine health. To rest, to wait. I am preparing you. I love you even when you don't love Me. You have a great deal of healing that must take place. You've taken steps backwards and away from Me. Release your anger with Me. Be ready for Me to counsel you. I will if you will let Me. You will be stronger. You will grow and you will desire to help others. Take My rest. It's yours for the taking. Let Me shower you with My love, the kind of love that lasts. The kind of love that no human can match."

DREAM TWO:

In this next dream, my friend Caroline and I were at an amusement park. We bought a ticket to observe a ride fourteen times. It was a roller coaster. If you paid to observe, you reclined on the ground, on your back under the track and watched other people ride right above your head. It felt dangerous. We got to watch so closely that it felt like we were on the ride.

I said to Caroline, "It feels like we are moving." She pointed out to me that, yes, we were moving — backwards. We had to keep inching our bodies further and further back because the track was getting lower each time riders would swoop above us.

If we stayed where we were, it would have crushed us. She reminded me several times we were moving backwards. The thirteenth time of watching, the track came so low it touched my legs. So, I pushed myself further backwards where it was safer.

Then, we had one more ride left on our ticket to observe. We decided to cut to the front of the line, hoping to use that last ticket (#14) to get on the ride. The male attendant saw us and said, "Go to the end of the line." It was far away. When I explained we had observer tickets and had one left, he said he'd consider letting us on. We'd have to wait and see if he would choose us. He wasn't sure. He said others were in line waiting with the same tickets. They decided they wanted to ride as well. It was up to this man if we got to ride our last ride or not. We just had to wait and see if we'd be chosen.

Interpretation:

I feel it's significant that this ride was supposed to be fun, but Caroline and I were just watching and stayed where it seemed safer. I think the roller coaster represented life—a life where we both felt stagnant, like observers and not participants. The longer we just watched, the more dangerous it got. It even required we move further back, which is also indicative of steps backwards in life. The longer we stayed off the ride (a.k.a. stopped living), the slower our progress would be. I think a roller coaster is a great metaphor for life; we must take the ups with the downs. It's not all easy and safe.

We did the right thing, having the courage to ask to get on the ride. Once we chose to give it a try, we had to wait. It was a consequence of our inactivity. We had to realize that just because we were ready didn't mean we could immediately start living, especially if someone else's choice was involved.

For example, the ride I chose to stay off for much of my life was dating relationships. Just because I decided I suddenly wanted to join the rest of the world and date didn't mean I could just go out and start doing that. I had to wait to be chosen. In Caroline's situation, she'd let some of her professional goals die for the sake of taking a safer, better paying job. Anytime she tried to go back and follow her dream profession, she was so far out of the job market, it was hard for her to break through.

This dream very much spoke to the states of both of our lives. We chose safety over facing fears; we chose to move backwards. When we chose to get back on the ride, we had to pay the consequences of being gone so long.

Those are just two examples of dreams I felt like God used to counsel me about my emotional condition. He supplied the picture of where I'd end up if I didn't change my choices.

Dreams give God an opportunity to speak where I am less likely to get in the way. God also has made it clear to me that while He does speak this way, sometimes I may have to wait for Him to reveal what He means by a dream's message. Sometimes, that answer comes through subsequent dreams. Sometimes, it comes through life. I get to watch and wait. Honestly, it's a true joy!

If hearing from God through dreams interests you, I encourage you to study more about how to understand the language of dreams. While a correctly interpreted dream can be healing, a wrongly interpreted one can be damaging. Let God and His Holy Spirit lead you in this, if you choose to start recording your dreams.

Again, it's important that you learn to hear God for your interpretation, rather than going to other people for their opinions. An exception would be if you are led to someone who has a gift for interpretation from God. I do not consider myself to be an interpreter of other people's dreams. I just know God has helped me understand mine.

God's Painted Pictures

God also can speak by supplying us with pictures and visions. Have you ever had a picture flash across your mind that was a snapshot of the condition of your heart? How about a picture that showed you where Jesus was working in your life? I've had God encourage me, speak truths to me, and instruct me through such pictures.

Here's an example. I wanted badly to be healed from depression over the end of a relationship. I ached so much to get to the end of my panic journey and finally be in a lasting, loving relationship. My depression was deep. I wanted out of either the depression or life, but I had no idea how to climb out of the darkness. I kept asking God (and anyone else who would listen) what I needed to do, as though it were one hundred percent up to me to fix myself. No matter what I tried, it failed. I couldn't shake the oppression and sadness within me. One time, while I was praying about it, I saw a picture in my mind's eye:

> **VISION:**
> *I saw Jesus walk up to the edge of a well. I saw myself at the bottom of this dark well. I was standing on a board that was attached to a rope that went all the way up to the top. I*

looked up to the top of the well where the only source of light
was. From the bottom of the well, all I could see was Jesus'
face. Then, He did all the arm work with the rope to pull me
out. My only instruction from Him was to not look back, not
look down into the darkness behind me. As Jesus was pulling
me out of the well, I locked my eyes with His. By the time He
pulled me up to the top, I noticed I had done none of the work.
He did it all! My only job was to keep my eyes on Him. Then
I felt the Lord say, "Keep looking up, not back, not down into
the deep hole that's below you."

I knew this picture was from God, showing me that I would not get over my depression if I kept dwelling on the past. He also was letting me know that it wasn't about me healing myself; it was about Him doing a good work in me.

During a different time of prayer, when my depression started to improve, Jesus finished that same vision for me:

VISION:

In the second vision, Jesus pulls me out of the well, His
right hand to my left arm. I am wet when I come out, smiling
when I reach the top where the sun lives. I was relieved and
happy to be out of the well. Jesus reminded me that He would
uphold me with His right hand.

Any time depression would try to overtake me I would meditate on these visions, reminding myself that Jesus is my strength. I'd tell myself not to look back on anything that could hurt me or set me back. It was so challenging, but that picture helped me. God gave me something tangible to ponder when I felt myself slipping backwards.

As the old saying goes, a picture is worth a thousand words. It's the pictures and images from God-given dreams and visions I recall throughout my day that speak volumes to me about my life. I encourage you to open yourself up to the possibility of God speaking to you through these means.

The next chapter will go in-depth through one of the most important methods for battling anxiety and fear: rewriting the lies we tell ourselves in our minds.

CHAPTER 10
A New Map:
Rewriting the Lies

What a man thinks of himself, that it is which
determines, or rather indicates, his fate.
(Henry David Thoreau)

Cheryl's Journal (December 31, 1995)
I am losing control. I am going to get sick, and everyone
will know it's a panic attack. I feel stupid for losing control
over a simple situation everyone else in the world lives
through just fine! Why can't I be normal? What is wrong
with me? I won't be able to think straight, to listen or
communicate. I'll close up and become incapacitated. Why
should I even try?

Encouraging, isn't it? That's a journal entry that captured the words
that flew through my mind before an episode of the *Watch Cheryl Panic
Show*.

Do these words sound familiar? It's no wonder that we work
ourselves into frenzies when we have no faith in our ability to cope,
when we speak to ourselves so negatively. Telling yourself you will fail

is a sure way to fail.

Why do we tell ourselves we're weak, worthless, and abnormal? Can we possibly find some new adjectives? (There are dictionaries full of them!)

Okay, so what's wrong with telling myself all those defeatist words? Do they build up my self-image? Do they help me? Of course not! Most importantly, they are lies. If I don't put up with listening to lies from other people, why on earth would I put up with them from myself? Yet, they became such a habit that I believed every word, every lie.

How can we rise above panic when we don't *believe* we can?

Are you a victim of the lies your mind feeds you? Our minds need to be retrained so we won't fall victim to the power of our thoughts. This is an important skill to master. It was key to my recovery!

This chapter provides a systematic rebuttal of lies, the armor we can put on when we feel an attack brewing. I will take the most common lies we tell ourselves and battle them with God's truth: truths from the Bible and truths God has revealed to me during prayer.

Importance of Beliefs

Before we get into rewriting the lies, we should examine the importance of internal thoughts and beliefs. As the Bible says in Romans 12:2 (kjv), you can be "transformed by the renewing of your mind." There are many wonderful books that discuss this subject at length. Therefore, I will just provide an overview about why it's important to reprogram our thoughts.

Malcolm Smith in *Freedom from Fear* recommends reprogramming how we think as a way to combat anxiety: "Even if we hate and cringe before what we tell ourselves, we obey it, believing that this is the way things really are…. It is impossible to add Truth to our hearts without having had a total change of mind concerning the Lie. The Truth cannot take root in soil that is under the control of the Lie…. Scientists tell us that we talk to ourselves in our mind at the equivalent of 1,300 words a minute..." (1)

Isn't that scary? Think of the damage we can do, if we dwell on the wrong 1,300 words every minute!

Are you convinced yet? I'd say the verdict is clear. Our thoughts contribute heavily to our anxiety problems, generating those physical symptoms. You know how we always want more control? Well, this is the one place we can gain control—our thoughts.

We need to take responsibility for the lies we think or speak and change them. I also recommend reading Derek Prince's *Blessing or Curse: You Can Choose*, where he helps us understand how we can pronounce curses over ourselves by speaking negative words. This chapter is about releasing us from the negativity we've brought into our lives through our mouths and our thoughts.

As we are about to rewrite the lies in our minds with the truths of the Bible, it is important to highlight a concept from Mark and Patti Virklers's *Prayers that Heal the Heart*. In their discussion of replacing negative expectations and beliefs with counter, positive beliefs, they emphasize the need for this to happen on the heart level where faith lives.

Our rewritten truths can't just be words we quote from memorization. The Virklers state that, "To replace my negative beliefs, I need more than a 'one-liner' from the Bible that states an opposite to my old belief system. It is not enough for my brain to memorize a new verse... I need a new faith. Faith is born in revelation, when God speaks to my heart, enlightening me to new insights from the Holy Scripture.... Saying a verse does not mean that you have revelation concerning that verse in your heart. People often say one thing while believing another. It is the revelation of God in your heart that changes your heart, not the words you parrot with your mouth." (2)

Don't Just Say It—Believe It!

Guess what? You no longer have to believe all those ugly lies you feed yourself! You can be free from the junk mail and false advertisements you've been listening to for so long. I don't want to live on lies anymore. Do you? If not, there's one thing you must do: *believe*.

While I can rewrite my lies here with the truths of the Bible, I need to *believe* the truth for them to have any affect on my thought processes and my body's reaction to a potential anxiety attack. You need to do this for yourself as you seek to replace the lies that go through your mind with God's truth. Don't feel that you need to rewrite each lie with a Bible verse. Be willing to place the lie before God and let Him rewrite it by speaking directly to your heart about the issue. For me, that can be just as effective as finding a Bible verse because it's personalized for me. You can do the same. God doesn't want you to believe the enemy's lies either; and God is more than happy to step in, grab a hold of that pen and write!

The Virklers say, "Don't use the mind to try to overcome the heart. Negative expectations in your heart must be overcome by revelation from God through the indwelling Holy Spirit who resides within your heart…. You must learn how to receive this revelation through the process of biblical meditation and through hearing the voice of God within your heart as you pray." (3)

Obviously, being able to hear and discern the voice of God is vital to our emotional health. Let the Holy Spirit be the Wonderful Counselor He's designated to be.

One day, I gave into the heap of negative words the enemy was more than happy to dish out, but then God stepped in and spoke to me about my tendency to think negative thoughts:

> *Cheryl's Journal (2003)*
>
> *God: Does focusing on what you consider to be bad encourage your spirit? Your spirit is a reflection of what you focus your heart and mind on. You focus on hurts and pain. Instead, focus on Me, My love, the amazing promises I've given to you, so your spirit can leap with joy. My voice is encouraging and boosting. Listen to My voice, not the voice*

of My enemy. You've heard him slander and shame you for too long. Tell him to be quiet and use My name with authority. You can do that! Do not let him defeat and overtake you and do not let any voice discourage you. Always tune to Me and My love instead as I bring peace, love, and joy into your life.

Hearing God speak directly to me builds my faith. I can take those words into my heart in the same way God illuminates a piece of Scripture and shows me how it personally applies to me. If you haven't made this a part of your relationship with God so far, seek to hear His voice.

ASSIGNMENT:
Make a list of all the lies you tell yourself:

Right before a full-blown attack:

During a full-blown attack:

(If you wrote the short story depicting what goes on inside your mind during an attack in Chapter 7, feel free to use it now to compile these lies.)

To follow is a list of the common words and phrases those of us who experience anxiety attacks say to ourselves before and during an attack. These are the types of lies we will rewrite with God's fresh words or battle with the truths of Scripture. For *The Lies, Set One*, I will refute each one with truths from Scripture. For *The Lies, Set Two*, I will share with you what I have learned during my journey or share revelation

God has given to me in times of prayer. I'll share God's guidance and revelation about my false beliefs.

THE LIES: (Set One)
Everything I tell myself, in my mind, is truth.

My life has no purpose.

Anxiety lives in me, and I can't get rid of it.

I suffer alone. I am alone in this.

No one is here to help carry this burden.

I have nowhere to turn for help.

God doesn't hear me crying. He doesn't care about me. He isn't listening to me. I am not important enough for Him to remember or think of me.

God has abandoned me.

There is no point to praying about this. It won't help.

I will never find the strength to overcome this.

I will never recover from anxiety.

Love is something to fear.

There is no place I can rest, no place I can recover from this.

If I worry, maybe the problem will go away.

Life isn't worth living. It's too much trouble.

I can't have peace.

God is not faithful.

God can't help me. I am beyond help.

THE LIES: (Set Two)
If anyone saw me for who I really am, they would reject me.

I'm not allowed to be anxious at all.

I am different; no one else has this problem. Other people are normal. Why am I the only one this is happening to? No one else is this stupid.

It's happening again. I can't stop it. It's more powerful than me. I look like an idiot, a fool.

I am out of control; I'm a failure when I can't control it. I must be in control always. I am not allowed to get sick.

I must be perfect. I can never make a mistake.

I've failed before; therefore, I will fail again.

I'm a helpless victim in this fight against my own body. There's nothing I can do to help myself.

I'm trapped with no way out.

I am not worth the trouble. No one will ever love me when I'm like this.

I must hide this from everyone. No one can know about this problem.

I must protect myself from pain.

If I brace myself and tense up, I can stay in control.

Refute the Lies with God's Word

Let's look at Set One, finding truths the Bible reveals about these lies. Having these truths has been helpful to me in times of anxiety. I wrote most of this list of lies during a season of my life when I'd been having many panic attacks. I wrote the truth segments during times of peace so I'd have a solid, biblical foundation to go to during times when I wasn't thinking clearly. I'd keep truthful verses on note cards in my back pocket to glance at when I needed them. I'd sling the truth back in the enemy's face to fight his deceptions.

THE LIES (SET ONE)

LIE: **Everything I tell myself, in my mind, is truth.**

TRUTH: Many lies that stream through our minds are from the devil himself, who wants us to be defeated. He is the author of lies.

John 8:44b: "[The devil] was a murderer from the beginning, not holding to the truth, for there is no truth in him. When he lies, he speaks his native language, for he is a liar and the father of lies."

The devil is the one who brings on fear, not God.

* * *

LIE: **My life has no purpose.**

TRUTH: Jeremiah 29:11: "'For I know the plans I have for you,' declares the LORD, 'plans to prosper you and not to harm you, plans to give you hope and a future'."

* * *

LIE: **Anxiety lives in me, and I can't get rid of it.**

TRUTH: We may feel like anxiety lives in us because it takes over our whole body. But it doesn't need to stay there. If we've asked Him to, we have a Savior who has taken up residence in our hearts.

Galatians 2:20a (kjv): "I am crucified with Christ: nevertheless I live; yet not I, but Christ liveth in me."

2 Timothy 1:7 (kjv): "For God hath not given us the spirit of fear; but of power, and of love, and of a sound mind."

* * *

LIE: **I suffer alone. I am alone in this.**

TRUTH: The Lord is right there with us whenever we endure any trial.

Isaiah 41:10, 13: "So do not fear, for I am with you; do not be dismayed, for I am your God. I will strengthen you and help you; I will uphold you with my righteous right hand…. For I am the LORD, your God, who takes hold of your right hand and says to you, 'Do not fear; I will help you.'"

Isaiah 43:2: "When you pass through the waters, I will be with you; and when you pass through the rivers, they will not sweep over you. When you walk through the fire, you will not be burned; the flames will not set you ablaze."

* * *

LIE: **I have nowhere to turn for help.**

TRUTH: Deuteronomy 33:27: "The eternal God is your refuge, and underneath are the everlasting arms. He will drive out your enemies before you, saying, 'Destroy them!'"

Psalm 27:1: "The LORD is my light and my salvation—whom shall

I fear? The LORD is the stronghold of my life—of whom shall I be afraid?"

Psalm 32:7: "You are my hiding place; you will protect me from trouble and surround me with songs of deliverance."

Psalm 32:8: "I will instruct you and teach you in the way you should go; I will counsel you with my loving eye on you."

Psalm 46:1-2: "God is our refuge and strength, an ever-present help in trouble. Therefore we will not fear, though the earth give way and the mountains fall into the heart of the sea."

Psalms 48:14 (kjv): "For this God is our God forever and ever: he will be our guide even unto death."

Psalm 118:6: "The LORD is with me; I will not be afraid. What can mere mortals do to me?"

Isaiah 58:11: "The LORD will guide you always; he will satisfy your needs in a sun-scorched land and will strengthen your frame. You will be like a well-watered garden, like a spring whose waters never fail."

Romans 8:31b: "If God is for us, who can be against us?"

1 Peter 5:7: "Cast all your anxiety on him because he cares for you."

* * *

LIE: **No one is here to help carry this burden.**

TRUTH: Joshua 1:9b: "Be strong and courageous. Do not be afraid; do not be discouraged, for the LORD your God will be with you wherever you go."

Isaiah 58:9a: "Then you will call, and the LORD will answer; you will cry for help, and he will say: Here am I."

Matthew 11:28: "Come to me, all you who are weary and burdened, and I will give you rest."

* * *

LIE: **God doesn't hear me crying. He doesn't care about me. He isn't listening to me. I am not important enough for Him to remember or think of me.**

TRUTH: Psalm 56:8a (kjv): "Thou tellest my wanderings; put thou my tears into thy bottle..."

Psalm 91:15: "He will call on me, and I will answer him; I will be with him in trouble, I will deliver him and honor him."

Isaiah 49:15b–16a: "I will not forget you! See, I have engraved you on the palms of my hands."

Matthew 10:30–31a: "And even the very hairs of your head are all numbered. So don't be afraid...."

2 Corinthians 1:3–4: "Praise be to the God and Father of our Lord Jesus Christ, the Father of compassion and the God of all comfort, who comforts us in all our troubles, so that we can comfort those in any trouble with the comfort we ourselves receive from God."

2 Corinthians 12:9: "But he said to me, 'My grace is sufficient for you, for my power is made perfect in weakness.'"

When we are weak, God has the chance to help us. When we admit to Him we can't do it on our own, He will come to our aid.

* * *

LIE: **God has abandoned me.**

TRUTH: Deuteronomy 31:6: "Be strong and courageous. Do not be afraid or terrified because of them, for the LORD your God goes with you; he will never leave you nor forsake you."

* * *

LIE: **There is no point to praying about this. It won't help.**

TRUTH: I like two translations of the same verse because of the different words used:

James 5:16b (niv) reads, "The prayer of a righteous person is powerful and effective." James 5:16 (kjv) reads, "the effectual fervent prayer of a righteous man availeth much."

There are many other verses that back up why we should pray:

Psalm 86:7 (kjv): "In the day of my trouble I will call upon thee; for thou wilt answer me."

Matthew 6:8b: "…your Father knows what you need before you ask him."

Matthew 7:7–8: "Ask and it will be given to you; seek and you will find; knock and the door will be opened to you. For everyone who asks receives; the one who seeks finds; and to the one who knocks, the door will be opened."

Mark 11:24: "Therefore I tell you, whatever you ask for in prayer, believe that you have received it, and it will be yours."

1 John 5:14: "This is the confidence we have in approaching God: that if we ask anything according to his will, he hears us."

* * *

LIE: **I will never find the strength to overcome this.**

TRUTH: It's true we can't find the strength to beat this on our own. It would be hard to manufacture that strength without the help of the Lord. However, we can let Him be the source of our strength.

Psalm 91:2: "I will say of the LORD, 'He is my refuge and my fortress, my God, in whom I trust.'"

Psalm 144:1–2: "Praise be to the LORD my Rock, who trains my hands for war, my fingers for battle. He is my loving God and my fortress, my stronghold and my deliverer, my shield, in whom I take refuge, who subdues peoples under me."

Isaiah 40:29: "He gives strength to the weary and increases the power of the weak."

Philippians 4:13: "I can do all this through him who gives me strength."

* * *

LIE: **I will never recover from anxiety.**

TRUTH: Jeremiah 30:17a: "But I will restore you to health and heal your wounds."

James 5:15a: "And the prayer offered in faith will make the sick person well; the Lord will raise them up..."

* * *

LIE: **Love is something to fear.**

TRUTH: We can miss out on a lot if we fight against love because we fear it.

1 John 4:18: "There is no fear in love. But perfect love drives out fear, because fear has to do with punishment. The one who fears is not made perfect in love."

* * *

LIE: **There is no place I can rest, no place I can recover from this.**

TRUTH: Exodus 33:14: "The Lord replied, 'My Presence will go with you, and I will give you rest.'"

Psalm 91:1: "Whoever dwells in the shelter of the Most High will rest in the shadow of the Almighty."

Proverbs 18:10: "The name of the LORD is a fortified tower; the righteous run to it and are safe."

* * *

LIE: **If I worry, maybe the problem will go away.**

TRUTH: In Matthew 6:25a, 27: "Therefore I tell you, do not worry about your life.... Can any of you by worrying can add a single hour to your life?"

* * *

LIE: **Life isn't worth living. It's too much trouble.**

TRUTH: Romans 8:18: "I consider that our present sufferings are not worth comparing with the glory that will be revealed in us."

2 Corinthians 4:17: "For our light and momentary troubles are achieving for us an eternal glory that far outweighs them all."

* * *

LIE: **I can't have peace.**

TRUTH: Isaiah 26:3: "You will keep in perfect peace those whose mind is steadfast, because they trust in you."

John 14:27: "Peace I leave with you; My peace I give you. I do not give to you as the world gives. Do not let your hearts be troubled and do not be afraid."

Philippians 4:7: "And the peace of God, which transcends all understanding, will guard your hearts and your minds in Christ Jesus."

* * *

LIE: **God is not faithful.**

TRUTH: 2 Thessalonians 3:3: "But the Lord is faithful, and he will strengthen and protect you from the evil one."

Hebrews 10:23: "Let us hold unswervingly to the hope we profess, for he who promised is faithful."

* * *

LIE: **God can't help me. I am beyond help.**

TRUTH: Psalm 121:1-2: "I lift up my eyes to the mountains — where does my help come from? My help comes from the LORD, the Maker of heaven and earth."

Psalm 138:8b: "...your love, LORD, endures forever—do not abandon the works of your hands."

Mark 10:27: "Jesus looked at them and said, 'With man this is impossible, but not with God; all things are possible with God.'"

Ephesians 3:20–21: "Now to him who is able to do immeasurably more than all we ask or imagine, according to his power that is at work within us, to him be glory in the church and in Christ Jesus throughout all generations, for ever and ever! Amen."

Hebrews 11:6: "And without faith it is impossible to please God, because anyone who comes to him must believe that he exists and that he rewards those who earnestly seek him."

Refute the Lies with God's Fresh Revelation

THE LIES (SET TWO)

To follow are more lies I've told myself while anxious. I will refute these lies with truths that I have learned in battling anxiety or with truths I felt God revealed to me during my prayer times.

LIE: **If anyone saw me for who I really am, they would reject me.**
TRUTH: I am a worthwhile person, a child of God. I am special. My worth comes from God alone, not others and their opinions of me.

* * *

LIE: **I'm not allowed to be anxious at all.**
TRUTH: Some degree of anxiousness is can be normal.

If you are feeling anxiety, ask yourself, "Is the amount of anxiety I feel normal to the situation?" Telling ourselves we can't have *any* anxiety will certainly produce even more anxiety. For example, first date jitters are normal. If I tell myself those jitters are wrong, I'm already making the situation worse. Demanding that I feel zero anxiety just won't work! (Haven't we tried that?) Sometimes, feeling anxious is warranted and by no means is an indicator that a full-blown attack is on its way.

* * *

LIE: **I am different; no one else has this problem. Other people are normal. Why am I the only one this is happening to? No one else is this stupid.**

TRUTH: No one is perfect.

Everyone has something they must deal with, something they wish weren't part of their lives. While it's true that not everyone has an anxiety disorder, we shouldn't feel insignificant or assume others are superior to us because they don't have this particular problem. Statistics show how extremely common this problem is!

When I prayed about these feelings, this is what I feel God said to me: "My daughter, do not speak poorly of yourself. Do not put yourself down. I am here to build you up. Every child of Mine is different. You are wonderfully made by My hand. You can find your restoration in Me."

* * *

LIE: **It's happening again. I can't stop it. It's more powerful than me. I look like an idiot, a fool.**

TRUTH: Anxiety is not stronger than me.

If I tell myself anxiety is more powerful, it will be even though it doesn't have to be. Rather than reprimanding myself because I can't stop it, it's better not to try to stop it. That only generates more anxiety. If I tell myself I'm allowed to be imperfect and that it doesn't matter if I get sick, it undercuts the power that anxiety has over me. Fighting against it generates more anxiousness. Calling myself names (like an idiot or a fool or a freak) has never been helpful. (Have you tried the insult method? Lovely, isn't it?) I usually just say to those thoughts, "Shut up!" You could even try to get sassy with it and say, "Shut your big, fat, hairy, ugly, lying trap!" If I do that enough times, my mind starts to listen (or I start laughing, which also relieves stress).

I feel the Lord also spoke to me about this lie, saying, "Come rest in Me. Look to Me for your peace and security. I will walk you through your anxieties. I do not always take the situation away, but I will hold your hand as you go through it. Do not run away. Embrace My hand as we walk together."

* * *

LIE: **I am out of control; I'm a failure when I can't control it. I must be in control always. I am not allowed to get sick.**

TRUTH: I am created by God. Therefore, I am not a failure no matter what I do or what happens to me. I don't have to be in control of my anxiety at all times. I need to surrender to God my desire to be in control of everything. God has told me more than once that He is the one in control. I don't have to be. (That's a relief!)

* * *

LIE: **I must be perfect. I can never make a mistake.**

TRUTH: God is the only perfect One. Being perfect is impossible for us. So, telling ourselves we have to do something that is impossible is setting ourselves up for failure and disappointment. Yet, in truth, we never had a chance to succeed with expectations like that.

* * *

LIE: **I've failed before; therefore, I will fail again.**

TRUTH: Just because we've struggled in the past does not mean we will struggle in the future. However, telling ourselves we will fail is a one-way ticket to anxiety doom! We need to believe we will get better. That all starts with how we talk to ourselves in our minds. Predict your success in your heart, not your failure.

I feel the Lord spoke to me and said, "What you believe in your heart is so important, My child. Do not let negativity and bad thoughts about yourself take root there. Your heart is precious. Fragile. It needs to be filled with faith in Me. Let's dig out all negative beliefs. The words you speak with your mind and state with your mouth will affect you. So, make those My truths."

* * *

LIE: **I'm a helpless victim in this fight against my own body. There's nothing I can do to help myself. I'm trapped with no way out.**

TRUTH: There is plenty we can do to help ourselves. We can be honest with whoever's around us about how we're feeling. We can give ourselves permission to leave a situation if it will help calm down an attack. We can move to a place where we are more comfortable until the feelings pass. We can give ourselves choices and not be helpless.

* * *

LIE: **I must hide this from everyone. No one can know about this problem.**

TRUTH: We *shouldn't* hide it. That only brings on more anxiety. We don't need to hide our imperfections. We also need to break down our pride.

God has encouraged me not to hide my problem. Writing this book is an exercise in this. God said to me, "I will use your pain. Be willing to share it with others. Do not hide. You are unapproachable when you hide your true self. I can use an open vessel who is willing to share from her heart. Be that vessel. Be willing to admit imperfections.

Do not demand of yourself what you cannot deliver. Do not demand more than I have asked of you. Others will be drawn to you when they see you are willing to drop the image of perfection."

* * *

LIE: **I must protect myself from pain.**

TRUTH: Hardships are a part of life. Everyone deals with them. We have to stop protecting ourselves from everything. Panic can make the scope of our world so much smaller if we let it take over by avoiding activities that bring on anxiety. We should avoid the temptation to protect ourselves too much. Are you letting fear rule your choices?

Regarding the issue of experiencing pain, God said to me, "I know there are times you wish I would have protected you from pain. I waste none of it. I use it for your good and My glory. Every time you have reason to shed a tear, the experience becomes one I can use. Every time you are pierced, you relate to someone new. Your life is not about you. It's about Me and those I want you to help. Do not shy away from pain and suffering. Expect Me to turn it into something for My glory."

* * *

LIE: **I am not worth the trouble. No one will ever love me when I'm like this.**

TRUTH: The people who love us will be able to accept us. Whoever can't accept our problems may not be the best people to lean on during anxious times. Just because one person may not be able to handle it does not change our value or worth.

God spoke healing into my heart over the rejection I'd experienced when people couldn't understand my problem. "My daughter, I am with you. I will never reject you. Some do not understand, but I understand. I know you inside and out. I am with you through every moment of this. You are walking through your healing with Me. Not everyone can join you on that journey, but I will never leave you."

* * *

LIE: **If I brace myself and tense up, I can stay in control.**

TRUTH: Bracing and tensing up will heighten your anxiety and aggravate physical symptoms. Stop trying to fight anxiety. Sometimes, speaking to your anxiety, welcoming it—as if to say, "bring it on"— undercuts its power. Have you ever *tried* to have an anxiety attack? See what happens. It's harder to have one when you're trying to than when you fight against it.

God's Peace Spoken

One day, I was praying about anxious feelings. I asked Jesus what I should do when I get anxious. This was His answer, spoken directly to my heart:

> *Jesus: "My peace I give to you. My peace I breathe into your life. I author the peace that passes all understanding, including your understanding. You can experience My peace when your eyes are locked with Mine. It's when you look around and focus on the circumstances that you don't have peace. Think of Peter who stepped out of the boat. When his eyes were on Me, he walked on water. But when his eyes strayed to the crashing waves around him, he sunk. He did the right thing, though, calling out to Me. If you ever feel yourself sinking, cry out to Me, reach up your hand and I will grab a hold of it. I'll hold you up in the storm. I may not always calm the waves around you. But if you keep your eyes on Me, you won't even notice them."*

I love when God, His Son, and the Holy Spirit speak such wisdom and truth into my life. I know whenever I've let lies from Satan creep into my heart and mind during anxious times, the last thing on my mind was keeping my eyes on Jesus, like the Lord suggests here.

We need to listen to God's calming voice. It can be challenging when the devil is shouting at us. Our enemy loves to plant those seeds of fear and doubt in us.

Think of it this way. If you opened your door and saw Satan standing there—yelling ridiculous, damaging words at you—what would you do? Would you invite him in? No! He has no right to enter your house and talk junk to you if you are a child of God. You don't even have to be polite. Next time he starts hurling accusations, picture yourself slamming that door in his ugly face. Then, continue the visualization. Go and sit down in a comfortable chair next to Jesus and ask Him what He'd like to say to you instead.

Attack Your Lies

Besides the lies that I have discussed here, you may have others that bombard your thoughts. Take the time to talk to God about them. Ask Him to rewrite them for you. Ask Him to give you a verse that He can make real to you in your heart, a verse that can help you change that lie into God's truth. Take the time to talk to God about these lies when you are in a calm state of mind, not during an attack. Read them over and over during calm times so you can start committing these ideas and principles to memory as well as making them a part of your belief system. They won't fail you when you need them, just like Jesus won't fail you when you need Him.

Cards of Encouragement

I've suggested keeping encouraging thoughts on note cards with you. Besides keeping Bible verses with me, I also wrote a summary of truths I could ponder during anxious times:

If I get sick, it's okay. I'm allowed.

I'll try to calm down, but if I have to, I can be sick.

I am not the only one who has this problem.

I'm allowed to do whatever I need to do to feel comfortable.

I do not have to hide anxiety.

I am a free person and free to make choices.

My needs are just as important as anyone else's.

I do not have to be perfect.

Some anxiety can be normal.

If I feel anxiety, it does not mean I will go into a full-blown panic attack.

I don't have to run away from a panic attack. I can and will live through it.

I can let go of whatever is not in my control.

Jesus is my strength.

Demonic Forces at Work?

Satan is the father of lies. We have unwelcome help when it comes to these lies growing in our hearts. Satan and his demons may play a significant role in the hopeless, fearful words we hear inside our minds. Demons could be whispering these thoughts and accusations. I encourage you to seek more information about deliverance from demonic pressures that may be contributing to your problem. I will give just a brief overview here.

Our beings have three parts: body, soul, and spirit. If we are Christians, our spirits cannot be possessed by demons. However, demons can trespass and trample on our bodies and souls if we open a door for them. Sometimes, the key to recovering is to pray this oppression away with the authority Jesus gave us to do so, and close any door we may have opened.

An excellent book on this topic is *Pigs in the Parlor* by Frank and Ida Mae Hammond. Jesus has given us authority to speak to these demons, call them by name and demand that they leave us alone. The Hammonds say, "Demons are spiritual enemies and it is the responsibility of each Christian to deal with them directly in spiritual warfare.... Satan's tactic is to put pressure on us. He does this in all areas of our thought life, emotions, decision-making and our physical bodies...but God's remedy for victory over demonic pressures is spiritual warfare.... The demons who are placed over various areas or territories are given authority to carry out whatever orders have been assigned. The Christian soldier need not be dismayed or discouraged...for the believer has even greater authority. He is vested with authority in the name of Jesus." (4)

During my healing process, I put a name on all negative pressures I felt needed to be prayed out. They included fear, anxiety, panic, mistrust, fear of rejection, perfectionism, inadequacy, self-loathing, shame, suicide, death, hopelessness, loneliness, depression, despair, bitterness, unforgiveness, resentment, and anger. These forces were far too present in my thoughts and in my life. I had to pray them out. I had to stop giving them room to harm me and to speak to my thoughts.

If these demons have no authority, why was I so oppressed by them? Because I had never told them to leave. As Jesus said in Luke 10:19, "I have given you authority to trample on snakes and scorpions and to overcome all the power of the enemy; nothing will harm you." You have the authority to call a demon by its name and tell him to go. That imp may put up a fight, but it's a fight he's already lost! He has no choice but to listen when you use Jesus' powerful name and plead the protecting blood of Jesus over yourself. You may have similar pressures hanging on to you that I did. Pray about this and ask God which pressures you need to pray out.

When Jesus taught us to pray, He included the petition: "Deliver us from the evil one" (Matthew 6:13b) Jesus acknowledged that believers need God's deliverance from the forces of the enemy. I encourage you to read more about this and get specific prayer for deliverance from the enemy's attacks in your life.

After that, put on the whole armor God outlined in Ephesians 6:10–18, so you can resist further onslaughts of the enemy. Visualize yourself putting on the helmet of salvation, protecting your thoughts, deflecting the arrows of the accuser.

As Proverbs 23:7a (kjv) reminds us, "For as he thinketh in his heart, so is he." Pay close attention to what your mind is feeding to your heart. It's key to overcoming anxiety.

Know what you believe.

Change it, if you believe in the wrong stuff. The wrong stuff doesn't get us anywhere. Believing God's truth can set us on the right path, toward His peace.

To follow is Chapter 11, a chapter I've prefaced many times throughout this book. It contains the most painful, yet one of my most necessary experiences in this whole journey towards peace. It was during this painful season God prompted me to write this book.

Journey with me through the time God asked me to face my biggest fear.

CHAPTER 11
Yield to God:
Face Your Biggest Fear

I believe that anyone can conquer fear by doing the
things he fears to do.
(Eleanor Roosevelt)

Has God ever started off a year prompting you to read the book of
Job? If He does, proceed with caution. Run for the nearest cave and
hide. Of course, you could try whining, "Do I have to, Lord?" I doubt
that will change anything, though. Most likely, God is preparing you
for something you don't want to face. For me, reading Job was
preparation for fire.

It was January 2003; God told me to read Job.

Everything around me seemed to be looking up. The year 2002
held much frustration. It lacked progress professionally and personally,
plus my relationship with God had gone stale. However, I always start
every year filled with hope, and 2003 had the makings of being an
awesome year. I could see much turnaround: Professional possibilities
abounded (after a recent unemployment). God started talking (well, I
was suddenly able to hear Him again). I also had a new relationship
brewing. My eyes looked with wonder toward what was sure to be an
amazing year!

That year was one of the worst years of my life.

However, by God's definition, He'd probably call it my best.

After God told me to read Job, He made a request of me in His still, small voice: "Get to know Me again."

And then, He asked me to face my biggest fear.

Giant-Sized Fears

Has God asked you to face your biggest fear yet? God asked me to get into the toughest, most daunting relationship.

To tell you this story, I must jump back to the end of 2001. In Chapter 8, I mentioned I started dating someone new one month after Richard.

Let's call him Andrew.

Andrew and I were set up through friends, so we didn't know each other when we started dating. We were great at communicating, but I could tell I wasn't getting the whole picture of who he was. When I started digging for more personal information, I got what I asked for: a truth about him that scared me, a challenge that didn't mix well with my insecurity, abandonment fears, and anxieties with men. I knew I'd drive him crazy if I tried to keep dating him.

To respect Andrew's privacy, I am not going to specify what made me fear being in a romantic relationship with him. I confided in him what my own problems were and why there was no way we could continue dating. Neither of us was emotionally involved, so it was a mutual decision to move on as just friends.

What was distressing to me was that I *had* to walk away.

Was I telling God I didn't have enough faith that He could heal me? Anxiety still held the reins on my life. I predicted my failure. I offered myself forgiveness; I felt like it was just too much to ask of myself because of the added challenges.

During 2002, Andrew and I built a beautiful, platonic friendship. Since we knew each other's secrets, we could talk about everything. Becoming real friends was fun for both of us. He grew to be one of the most important men I've ever had in my life.

For the first time, I could be open and honest without embarrassment. I could admit imperfections to a guy. This healthy friendship gave me a chance to grow.

Then, January 2003 rolled around with God's assignment to read Job and a directive for me, from God, to face my biggest fear:

I was lying in bed one Sunday night. (Incidentally, this was right after I returned from a frustrating singles retreat from church, with a fellow, equally frustrated, single girl.) Out of nowhere, inside, I heard God say to me:

"It's time to give Andrew another chance."

I sat straight up in bed and gasped, "What? Are you crazy?"

I knew this suggestion had to come from God because it would never have come from me. I said, "Do I have to? You know why that particular relationship is too scary for me." God told me what He always tells me when I try to get out of something because of fear:

"Do it anyway."

As far as I knew, the two of us didn't like each other that way. I didn't see how this could work. I was so afraid this situation could bring panic on full-force. What if I undid all of my hard work, putting myself through a relationship that had a good chance of hurting me? I couldn't believe God was asking me to do this. But, alas, He was.

That is so like God.

I gave God a list of three things He had to do before I'd be willing to take this risk. Thinking God doesn't usually give into our demands, I figured I was grounded on the safe side of fear.

I figured wrong.

God performed all three, quickly, I might add. (Sometimes God can be annoying, eh? Especially since He never seemed to do anything else fast on my behalf!)

During my time of seeking God about this, Andrew and I were working together on a romance video series for his church. We interviewed longtime couples about what makes marriages last. Their words echoed everything Andrew and I said we were looking for in our future spouses. These people would nearly quote the words we had just said to each other. I thought, *God, are you trying to send me more hints, clues, messages?*

I wondered if Andrew was picking up on any of that. (I found out later he was!) When Andrew and I shared with each other what we were looking for, I tried not to freak over our nearly identical "lists." (You know, that wish list of what you want in a spouse. Mine was laminated. Just kidding, of course!)

I figured Andrew would never approach me about a relationship, considering I told him the last time it would never work. I felt the responsibility rested on me. Yet, how on earth was I supposed to approach this subject—with a guy friend—when I had no clue what he thought of me? Talk about nerve-racking!

Yes, God loves asking us to do the scary stuff. I asked Andrew if we could get together, not telling him why I wanted to talk to him. The night before, I wrote in my journal:

> *Cheryl's Journal (February 10, 2003)*
> *Lord, more than anything, I want to have this conversation without panic attacks. I don't mind a few nerves; they're normal. But I want to know I've grown through all my work. I want to see fruits of my years of labor. I know where my problem came from. I know I am in no physical danger from this person. I don't want to need pills. I want to walk through my healing and grow in it. How will I react? Will I be awful like in 1996 with Nathan? Will I freak out and have panic attacks? Will I destroy the relationship because I'll display a lack of trust?*

Nothing tells us for certain we'll be fine. Nothing tells us we won't have an anxiety attack just because we've done much work. But still, I had to step out in faith and test myself and see what would happen.

Finally, it was time for the big talk. I'll admit I was nervous. But who wouldn't be, approaching a friend about whether he had any feelings beyond friendship? I told myself, *Cheryl, it's acceptable to feel nervous. This is not a sign that panic is back. I mean, think about what you're doing! Actually, don't think. It will only make you more nervous. You're a little nutty to take this risk.*

I used a few of my coping methods. I fought negative thoughts with God's truths. I also told myself, *Hey, if you get sick, you get sick. It's no big deal! Not the end of the world.* I did focus on breathing a few times when it seemed too shallow. I even visualized the positive way the situation could go, imagining myself calm. (And yes, I had fun imagining his response would be good — oh, the nice words he said to me in my imagination! What can I say? I'm a writer; I write the life I wish for in my head.)

When we started the conversation, to undercut the anxiety, I admitted to him right away I was nervous. My wonderfully accepting friend made me feel like that was okay. But guess what? No anxiety attack came. I never had to run away from the table to throw up.

When I asked him if he figured out what I wanted to talk about, he said, "I hope it's the same thing I want to talk to you about." Then, I knew it was mutual. I knew I didn't have to put myself on the line with a friend who didn't feel the same way.

Andrew wanted to take our relationship to the next level as well, stating he wanted to enter a courtship to figure out if we were compatible for marriage. I was pleasantly surprised he'd thought it through that far already and was taking this seriously.

Then, I had to warn him; I had no idea how my anxiety problems would be. Now my heart was involved. The same dangers that were there the first time we dated still existed. I didn't know how I'd be or how my body would react to the risks. I had to make sure he realized the fun friend he knew might change before his eyes.

With every ounce of his being, he convinced me that he was completely okay with the fact that I might not always be. He promised patience. He even wanted to learn more about my problem so he could understand me better. He was, by far, the most understanding boyfriend I'd ever had!

Is This the Light at the End of the Tunnel?

Was the end of my anxiety problem in reach? Getting into this relationship with Andrew made me feel like it was! I thought, *maybe he's the last man I'll have to get used to, so I can put my panic disorder behind me.*

For the next couple of days, I felt myself going through a transition, emotionally: from anxious to excited. My appetite returned. The next time I saw Andrew, I surprised myself by being able to eat. Even as I was doing it, I said to him, "I don't know why I'm okay, but I am. I hope it continues." He kindly said, "I'm glad you're okay, but if tomorrow you're not, that's okay too."

I celebrated that night's victory in my journal:

> *Cheryl's Journal (February 13, 2003)*
> *I got to see Andrew tonight. I even ate with him, comfortably. I can't believe I didn't need pills. What an amazing thing! And it was the first time seeing him after our newly established relationship. God, I can feel You working. I can feel the reprieve from all the pain. I can feel panic leaving my existence. I want to use tonight's success as a launch pad for all future successes. Lord, I feel Your hand in this whole situation. I feel I'm finally experiencing what I've missed all these years.*

Within days, my anxieties were gone, and I was comfortable with Andrew. A year before, I told God that I'd never survive this particular relationship; God set out to prove me wrong. For the first time in my adult life, I had a boyfriend for Valentines Day. We made the most of celebrating that day and our new relationship, redeeming all the previous lonely ones. It was the night we shared our first kiss.

The Romance

This was the first relationship in which I gave myself permission to break down my protective barriers and allow my heart to get truly involved. It was exhilarating and scary at the same time. I welcomed every bit of it because I felt like I had missed out my whole life. I had missed the experience of falling in love. I felt this was safe because God so clearly led us both into this relationship.

My relationship with Andrew was an adventure. Because we shared so much already going into it, we had nothing to hide. The openness between us was unlike anything I'd ever had. I felt closer to him than any man.

We had such an amazing time, experiencing both fun and tender moments that go along with moving through a courtship. Early on, we started a courtship study, a pre-engagement book to help us see compatibilities, differences, strengths, and weaknesses within the relationship. We talked about which strengths we both brought into this, where the other made up for weaknesses.

Much of our relationship was intense and rooted in talking through serious issues; yet, it seemed with each talk we grew closer. I felt like I was communicating with someone on the deepest level I could. I admired both of us for being able to do this, as neither of us had been able to do that before.

We'd pray together, talk about God for hours on end, and also spend lots of time just playing together. We had so much fun sharing in all sorts of adventures: train trips, hiking trips, taking in new sites, experiencing new places. We always made a big deal about celebrating our monthly anniversaries; each one was an important milestone. I know for me, each one furthered my healing, my walk toward wholeness.

Okay, now here is where I blush. This relationship was also a chance for me to feel comfortable with the affections of a man. Finally. As I shared in Chapter 6, in the past, moving from a friendship to a romantic relationship triggered anxiety because of the more intimate nature of romance. I want to be clear that Andrew and I set our boundaries well within God's plan, never going beyond where we felt God's blessing. God was the One who brought us together. God was the center of our relationship, and we carefully prioritized pleasing Him in the way we expressed ourselves physically with each other. Our commitment to purity understood, I can hardly articulate how exciting it was to feel at ease expressing what was growing in my heart in this way. To do so without anxiety was such a miracle for me!

I distinctly remember one evening we shared an intimacy that touched my heart. We started off the evening at a romantic restaurant. Afterward, we snuggled to the scenes of *Casablanca*. (In a travesty of sorts, I had never seen the movie, and Andrew wanted to share that experience with me.) Later, it seemed the walls I'd put up between myself and intimacy with another person were finally down. I was able to walk in healing from the brokenness of my past. We shared a time of deep, mutual trust, a time so precious that made it difficult for me to leave his home that night. (But of course, I did. Had to stick to those boundaries!) Those moments touched me so much that I actually started crying. That had never happened to me in a "good" way. Andrew just held me and didn't even need to ask if they were good tears or bad tears; he just knew. It was the night I started to fall in love with him — that wonderful feeling that I had never felt in my life. The glow of this special time stayed in my heart for days. Have you ever felt that before, where an experience lasted long after the moment had ended?

To follow is an entry I wrote in praise to God:

Cheryl's Journal (April 2, 2003)

I am on a track for victory. I started organizing notes for my Panic book, not knowing if I would ever get to a point of victory, the point where I could even publish it with confidence that it's actually a success story. The point that made me feel like there was light at the end of the dark tunnel.

But today, as I write this, I am in the middle of one of the biggest anxiety victories of my life. It makes me feel like this problem is behind me. I never thought it would be. But I've watched the amazing, capable hand of God working in my life. Yes, I had to go through many years of hard work to get to this point, but finally, I feel like I am experiencing a real healing.

Of course, as with any relationship, it was not without its challenges. Any time I felt anxiety creeping in, I immediately ran straight to God. I leaned on Him and let Him counsel me. God met me where I was every single step of the way.

Most of the relationship with Andrew was really positive, so positive I believed we'd get married. Close to three months in, we completed our first pre-engagement study. There were no red flags or problems. We asked all the right questions to evaluate our compatibility. We decided we were ready to move on to our second, more serious pre-engagement study. My excitement grew with each step we took in a positive direction.

Then, a week later, Andrew let me know he thought I was too far ahead of him in feelings and that I needed to slow down. He also told me it would be a good time to start "guarding my heart."

Well, his warning came far too late. I was already in love with him. I hadn't told him because I didn't want to pressure him. I was devastated because I had no idea he was so far behind me. I thought he was just as invested as I was. That talk—from my point of view—came out of nowhere.

Andrew assured me he still wanted to be in the relationship; he just wanted a chance to catch up to me. It was hard for me to stay; all of my security had been rocked. I had no idea how I'd survive this new volatility. The first week after that talk was really hard, yet I still, miraculously, had no panic attacks.

Then, for our three-month anniversary, Andrew went out of his way to surprise me and make me feel at rest about us. He was truly sensitive to the fact that those talks stirred up much anxiety in me. To celebrate us, he didn't say where we were going; he just told me to dress warmly. The rest of the night unfolded his thoughtful surprises.

First, he knew during anxious times, I love to be outside by the ocean where there are calming waves, a soothing breeze. (And air! Air is always good in times of anxiety!) Second, this man, who was an amazing listener, was sweet enough to remember what I told him, months earlier, was my idea of the perfect date: a picnic on the beach in time for the sunset. Andrew gave that night to me. He had hidden all my favorite foods in the trunk of the car. (I'm a little dense. The slight aroma of food didn't even give his surprise away!) Thankfully, his warm gestures calmed me enough to enjoy this meal by sunset. Once the sun went down, the stars were so clear above. We talked well into that beautiful night. That's when he gave me the most meaningful gift. It was a card in which he had written something that meant the world to me. He wrote that I was a treasure to my Lord and to him.

As I mentioned in previous chapters, I had gone my whole life never feeling treasured or chosen by anyone. These words touched me to the core; they were exactly what I needed, to give me the courage to stay in the relationship and not run away. There was no way to put my defenses back up; it was too late for that. I had to keep on loving, keep on risking.

Warning Signs of the End

Has God ever warned you before something bad was about to happen?

This was when God started to speak to me through dreams. That hadn't happened to me before. Well, not that I'd noticed. So I didn't recognize that God was speaking.

God sent me eight dreams, all with one message: Andrew would walk away from our relationship. However, I firmly believed since God brought us together that we were going to get married. Surely, God would not have led me down this path, only for it to end on me.

But again, all eight dreams were a warning. They were the voice of God, trying to prepare my heart.

I passed off the dreams as my anxiety talking. I didn't realize at the time that God still speaks through dreams. I didn't know I should pay attention. Five of those dreams came during a trip to Florida that Andrew and I took so he could meet my family. Everything was going well on the trip, yet I kept having nightmares that were telling me otherwise.

When I wasn't getting God's point through the dreams, God decided to send me a message another way. A wonderful friend—who for over twenty years has been gifted in the Holy Spirit with words of prophecy—gave me God's warning that my relationship with Andrew would be ending.

I was devastated!

I was finally in love with someone who could handle the anxious part of me, finally able to let someone in. How on earth could this be happening? Why would God do this to me? Right when I thought this problem was behind me, Andrew was going to be ripped away. This meant, yet again, I'd have to start all over with someone else, trying all over again to be okay, not panic, and learn to trust a new man.

I didn't tell Andrew what God had revealed to me. I had to wait one long week for what God warned me about to happen. I had to do nothing, not act like I was going crazy inside, and wait for it to happen. I knew a week before Andrew did, what his decision would be about our relationship, a decision he hadn't verbally told me he was trying to make.

It was a Sunday afternoon when Andrew broke up with me, days before our fourth month anniversary. I would have been beyond devastated if God hadn't warned me. Instead, though it was difficult, I was prepared, expecting it. I'm thankful my loving God prepared me. That's proof of God's amazing ways to me, even though the news was painful.

At first, Andrew's explanation about why he wanted our

relationship to end didn't sit right with me; I didn't feel like I was getting the real story. I pressed him for an answer that would help me understand. I got what I asked for. Perhaps I shouldn't have pressed and should have just let it go. However, I know myself! I would have wasted so much time wondering what the real reason was, writing my own excuses for why he wanted out. I would have damaged my self-esteem by contemplating all the possible things that could be wrong with me. I needed to know so I could accept it then move past it. I say this in Andrew's defense that he absolutely would not have told me the following, had I not asked for the real reason. Nevertheless, his answer took me a long time to heal from because it dug into the wound I'd been trying to heal from my entire life — the wound that told me I wasn't a treasure.

The bottom line was Andrew was not in love with me and didn't think he ever would be. He said he'd been seeking God about me, praying the verse in Matthew 6:21 that says, "For where your treasure is, there your heart will be also." He'd been praying for God to make me a treasure to him so he could love me, but that never happened. It was time, for my sake, to give up trying. Since I had taken the words he wrote to me on our third month anniversary to heart, it made this reason for the breakup all the more excruciating. These words were the arrows that struck me the deepest; they took me the longest to get over. Later in this chapter, I'll show you how God healed me of this.

The Huge Setback

Was my anxiety disorder coming back? The week leading up to the end was wrought with much anxiety and no appetite. I claimed defeat, swearing anxiety had come back, that I was no better. I decided to throw away the pieces I had started toward writing this book, vowing that I had nothing to say about getting healed because I wasn't better. I was down to 112 pounds, almost as bad as I was in 1990, around the time I ended up in the hospital.

I thought I had experienced a huge setback.

Thank God I was wrong.

It's important to be able to distinguish between unreasonable anxiety associated with a disorder and anxiety that is appropriate for a situation. My anxiety was actually grief that I mistook for my disorder acting up. I realized by definition, an anxiety disorder is categorized by an unusual amount of fear over something that isn't dangerous. My first panic attacks before dates or during a dance were classic examples of this.

However, in this case, there was emotional danger. I was losing a man I loved with all my heart and soul. It encouraged me to realize it was not a setback in my anxiety healing. Instead, I was able to grasp that I had just completed a high-risk relationship without having a single panic attack. That was something to celebrate! So, what I thought was a setback turned into a victory.

I suggest you practice discernment when you feel anxiety. Ask yourself: "Is there a reasonable basis for feeling the way I do?" Don't assume all anxiety is bad. Don't assume feeling anxiety will grow into a panic attack.

And remember: we're only human.

The anxiety I felt was a human emotion from losing an important relationship. I didn't need to beat myself up for feeling it. (That never helps anyway, does it?) If I hadn't forgiven myself for being human, I could have invited anxiety to reenter my life in unhealthy ways.

It was devastating to me that this man wasn't the end of my journey with panic, but he was my biggest, anxiety success story. I couldn't deny his role in my healing no matter how much pain my love for him caused me.

Detour to Depression

Have you ever found yourself down a dark hole, not having a clue how to climb out? Depression hit me hard, a long, dark period of my life where I had my most volatile relationship with God ever! I was angry. Hurt. Bitter. You name it. I felt it! I just couldn't understand what God was thinking when He drove me straight into that relationship, only for me to fall flat on my face, left in the wake of misery.

Life got terribly dark after the breakup. It seemed like so many challenges piled on me at once. It is not the purpose of this book for me to spill all the hard times I experienced. Just trust me when I say I felt like Job, like God was allowing much affliction to enter my life while He was just standing there watching.

On top of trying to mourn such a huge loss, my family experienced major challenges, I struggled with my health, unemployment, and unfulfilled writing promises and opportunities. I was told by trusted mentors that I should give up writing, that I might never be good enough. Writing was all I had left, and even that was under attack. Everything fell apart in four weeks' time. Absolutely nothing was going right; I had nothing to live for.

Have you ever begged God to just take your life? I did, over and over. I didn't want to live anymore; I didn't see any point. The words "just kill me now, God" came out of my mouth daily. I might have been able to handle the other challenges had I not just suffered such a huge relationship loss. All of those things thrown on top of a deep grief felt to me like God was allowing too much.

And let's not forget how I got into this mess!

I chose to obey God. I listened to His call to give this guy another chance. Look what God allowed to happen! He let me down, and He was not there to pick up the pieces.

Or was He?

Well, there's no doubt God was there, but He wasn't following my instructions. He was there to shape me, mold me, to grow me up in Him, no matter how painful.

The Virklers define depression as, "giving in to the pressures of life, while letting go of our faith in God. Depression is the direct result of listening to the wrong voices and focusing on the wrong vision. When I listen to the lies of the accuser and stop my ears to the comfort and wisdom of the spirit of God, I have started down the road of depression." (1)

It didn't matter how many promises God had made to me by this point about my future. Plus, His biblical promise in Romans 8:28, that "all things God works for the good" meant nothing to me. I was in pain, and that's where my eyes and heart were focused. That's what contributed to keeping me down. However, God did continue to speak.

God Speaks Direction

The only reason I held on to life during that season was that God spoke clearly, often, in various ways. He'd speak through dialoguing, visions, and dreams. In the Appendix, I've supplied some of the large amounts of journaling I did throughout this relationship and its aftermath. I'm sharing with you both my journaling and outcries to God, as well as some of God's responses back to me through dialoguing. In this chapter, I'll include a few slices of this.

One night, after I begged God to let me die, these were the words He spoke to my heart:

Cheryl's Journal (January 15, 2004)

You wake up each day, Cheryl, because I am not through with you yet. Yes, you've felt pain. Yes, you've endured a lot. It's all preparation for what I have in store. You will not go to those depths again. You can celebrate with Me now. There is so much ahead. I get to see it. I know you can't yet, but I do. I have that vision of your future. You would be overwhelmed if I let you peek. You don't need to peek. You are just to trust in Me, your God, your Savior, your Friend, your Counselor. Lean on Me as we continue to walk together. Let go of uncertainty. I am your certainty. Trust in Me. I know what's best, and I am leading you down the best pathway because you have remained open to Me and My calling. I have a very specific calling for your life.

One of the coolest things God did for me during this season was talk directly to me, then confirm the same words through someone else. I would keep God's words to myself, then a friend would give me the same message from God. I know that was His way of showing me I was hearing Him correctly. It helped me to not doubt; it helped me accept His healing words. It made it easier to trust and believe God's counsel.

To follow is another entry of God's word spoken to me:

> *Cheryl's Journal (January 24, 2004)*
> *Take in My Word and My promises daily. Stand on My promises. Believe them. Recite them until you believe them. I will hold your hand if you will let Me. You must be open. Stop closing that door. No other intimacy will complete you like My intimacy. No relationship survives without trust. Count Me trustworthy, even when I lead you down paths of pain. It will make sense to you one day. I promise you will see purpose. Don't choose death. Choose Me. Lean on Me in this season of great pain, and I will fill you. I will complete you, teach you, and guide you. I thwart your plans. Go with Mine. Release yourself to Me, and trust Me again. Do not blame Me for everything that goes wrong. Life has its ups and downs. Following Me means accepting My plans, even when you don't know what they are. For your ways are not My ways. Your plans are not My plans. Stop fighting against what I set in motion. Go with Me, not against Me. I will not lead you astray.*

I hope you can see how God can be our Counselor in such a mighty way through the words He speaks to our hearts. Have you asked God to counsel you through your anxiety disorder? How I wish I had known how to hear Him during all those years!

Here's another example of God's counsel:

Cheryl's Journal (January 16, 2004)

There is no fear when you risk for Me. I will equip you and sustain you, even when you don't feel qualified. I am the One who gives you strength. I can blossom you, even in the most unlikely circumstances. You also have to step out of the boat and be willing to risk. Be willing to trust Me. Be willing to let Me use you. Keep your eyes focused on Me and only Me. Know that it's My eternal kingdom that matters, not this world and its passing things. Even a broken heart will not matter in the eternal realm. Those things are passing, those hurts and disappointments. There will come a day when they will be like dust under your feet. I can blossom you when you give Me your life to use for My glory. I can use you in different ways you hadn't imagined. I need you to let go of your own hedge of protection, and let Me protect you in My ways. That means leaving comfort zones, trying new things. With Me by your side, there is no danger to you eternally. I never leave your side. I am with you always. I never promised comfort or an easy life. Actually, I promise hardship, challenge, and change. Following Me is a choice, and following Me means facing challenges. I will never lead you into a situation that isn't for your ultimate good. You can trust in Me and in what I know about you. I know you better than you know yourself. I knew you before you were born. I know the number of hairs on your head and the day that you will die. You don't need to know the blueprint, as I am the Keeper of such things. Your only instruction is to trust, to step out of that boat and let Me use you.

Have you noticed how God had to tell me similar things, over and over? Well, it's probably because I asked Him the same questions, over and over: why He wanted this pain for me, why He asked me to walk through that door. For months, it's all He heard from me. I completely regretted obeying Him.

During this challenging season, I begged God to give me something to hold onto: a writing assignment, a job, or a new boyfriend (even though I was too hurt to try again). I begged for something to distract me from all the pain. Guess how God responded to that one? He informed me that He is not a God of distractions and that I needed to take the season to heal. (He really is the Divine Thwarter of all my plans!)

Wrestling Match

Have you ever wrestled with God? I think wrestling is a normal part of close relationships. This was the year I had the most volatile, yet deepest relationship I've ever had with God. If you think about Christ coming back for us, His bride, we are in an engagement with Him. Engagements require communication, patience, work, understanding, and yes, even fights. That defines my year with the Lord in the wilderness.

I finally had a true engagement — with God. And it hurt! But it was the most important year I've ever had with God. And you know what? That's reason enough to go through all that pain. (Well, that's easier to say at the back end of it. I certainly didn't always feel that way!)

As humans, we'll never understand God. The truth is God may not want to communicate about what we want to discuss, at least not at the moment we ask. He knows the right time to give us an answer. When He chooses not to answer or to delay an answer, it's for our benefit. It's hard to face that silence when we ask a question. Derek Prince, in *Blessing or Curse: You Can Choose* says, "It is vain for us to seek to pry God's secrets from Him. It is also irreverent. If God withholds an answer, it is more important for us to trust than to understand." (2)

God isn't a puppet who answers to our demands. He is so much more than that. He knows someday we'll understand. (Or perhaps by then — like when we're in His presence — we really won't care because we'll see that what matters is God and who we are in relation to Him for eternity.)

A Time to Grieve

When I stopped trying to fight what I was going through (and stopped begging God to just take the pain away), I realized I needed to give myself permission to grieve. This was the first time I'd ever fallen in love with someone. I remember shortly after the breakup, I wrote in my journal, "It's been three weeks! Why am I still crying?"

If I'd known it was going to take eight months to stop crying, I probably would have given up, right then and there. This was a journey I had to walk; I had to walk it with God alone. He wasn't going to just take my love for this person away without me going through the mourning process. (But believe me, I asked Him for that! He unequivocally said no.)

I used this emotional experience to grow by not hiding my pain. I chose not to pretend for the sake of others being able to see me as strong. As you know, I spent countless years pretending, putting on the fake "I'm okay, nothing hurts me" mask. I refused to do that this time. Some people resisted this in me, wanted me to just get over it. I knew I had to deal with it in full, so I could move on to be an emotionally healthy person.

I must say that during the whole grieving process, my parents were amazing. They stepped up and helped me through this emotional time. To think—all of my teen life—I hid my emotions from them! Finally telling them about the abuse put down a solid foundation that allowed me to be transparent with them through this grieving process. This gave them the chance to truly be there for me during one of the most difficult seasons of my life. Their love and support helped me hang on to life. For the first time in my life, I wasn't embarrassed to admit to them that I hurt.

My aunt, Jackie, was also a huge support. While she ached for me and my pain, she also expressed how proud she was that I'd finally been able to fall in love with someone. She helped me see the good side of the pain I was going through; I had finally broken down the protective barriers around my heart.

When I went home for Christmas 2003 to visit family and friends, a friend's father pointed out to me that he was amazed by how different I was—how suddenly I had joined the human race. I had blossomed into a person who no longer put on a show or a perfect image, a person who had finally become real. He saw it as a sign of strength and growth, not weakness, that I was willing, finally, to admit hurts and pains. (He's known me since I was eleven years old.)

The trusted mentors in my life helped me see the whole year wasn't a waste. I was learning the life skills I needed. And when does that not come through pain?

I never, ever want to live from a place where I tell myself I don't have permission to feel when I suffer a loss. Pretending is too stressful, too draining, and it's a lie that I don't want to live anymore! And sometimes this also means pouring out my complaints to God. And guess what? He can take them!

At first, I didn't think there could ever be a logical explanation about why all the pain was necessary, why God led me straight into pain. But then, I realized I had to face my biggest fear to advance toward the end of my healing journey, that final destination called peace. God also showed me in a million ways how He walked with me for every single step of this whole situation.

An Honest Cry, An Honest Answer

To follow is a journal entry, a true outpouring to God. In it, I go back and forth between trust and bitterness, between anger with God and clinging to Him.

Remember! I don't always believe everything I say in my journals. My outpourings are truthful at the time I write them. But when I go back and read them later, I find I write out of my pain and not truth.

The following entry shows a shift in my thinking by its end.

Clearly, God was with me that day on the Pacific Coast sand when I wrote this:

Cheryl's Journal (January 25, 2004)

Lord, I'm at the end of things emotionally, yet somehow I still come to you. What is it You want from me? I don't have any strength left to fight. God, You are the only One with any power here. I've failed miserably, trying on my own. I may not know how to trust You, but I can learn again. It may take time. I believe I won't progress personally or professionally or with relationships until I can let go of my anger with You. But it makes me feel like I'm being bribed. You have all control; I have none. Nothing will happen in my life until I accept that. I seriously struggle with this. Well, maybe it's significant You are working on me so much. Maybe it's because I've been willing to be used by You. Maybe You're sharpening me into a vessel You can use, but that sharpening causes pain. I guess the questions I need to ask myself are: Do I want to be used by God? Do I want to be in a shape He can use? Am I malleable enough for Him? Will I walk where He wants me to walk? In truth, I wouldn't know how not to follow God. I don't have anything else. No plans. No agenda. It's not like I've chosen one road for my life when God's chosen another. It's not like we're fighting over it. I'm not at a crossroads, except maybe the one that would ask: Do I want to be a Christian anymore? What's the alternative? What's my backup plan? What would I be choosing over God? The plain truth is nothing. So again, I find myself at God's mercy, the One who holds all control. When did I get so helpless? I guess the circle of our journeys must take us back to one thing: God and the control He has. I am grieved that God isn't moving on my pain. He's inflicting it. Perhaps He's like the doctor who knows the only way to rid me of this "tumor" is to cause me much pain. Without that pain, maybe I'll never heal of the "cancer" eating away at me. Kids never understand when their parents bring them in for shots. The small pain now saves that child a great deal of pain later. Kids can't see the big picture, much like we can't. I am God's kid; God sees it all. He knows what He's doing, what He's saving me from. He sees. And He knows what He's saving me for, _who_ He's saving me for. He sees it all and asks me to trust Him to hold my big picture in His hands. I want to, Lord, oh, how I want to say it and mean it! Feel it! Help me to do just that.

To follow is God's response after my outpouring:

God: I am the Peace in the midst of a storm. I give reason to the unexplainable. Yes, I think of the big picture. I see it. I act in your best interests. I know a small amount of pain, now, saves you from more, later. I saved you from death. I died for you. I sacrificed for you. I love you. I watch over you. I ride the good and bad waves with you. I steer you in the right direction. I know what's best for you. I've designed a perfect will for your life. I know what you really need. I am to be your all. In the end, I am all that matters. All this pain is but dust under your feet. One day, it will be a faded memory. One day, it won't sting. One day, you will shine and rise above. Cling to Me, and it can be soon. I have not left you alone. Welcome Me to gut this out, to clean this up. Let Me counsel you in My wise ways. Surrender to Me. Give Me your exhaustion, your pain, the last bit of control you're trying to hold onto.

God's Treasure
After this outpouring, my depression started to lift. There was still one

painful arrow lodged deeply into my heart: being told I wasn't a treasure. I needed God to heal me of this. I had already struggled, starting out my young life as a victim of abuse where I was not protected, not treasured, and instead, violated by someone.

I spent years floundering, feeling like I had no place in this world. I never felt like I belonged with anyone, never felt like I fit in. I felt no one would ever love me enough to accept me—faults and all. This breakup with Andrew worsened those insecurities, sent a message to my heart that I was right to have those insecurities. I believed no one would ever see me as a treasure. I didn't know how to undo that damage to my heart. God knew how; God knew this would take surgery with His God-sized scalpel to make me well again.

Around the time of the breakup, two people came to me separately with messages from God. I hadn't told either of them what was said to me regarding a treasure. One message was the verse Proverbs 3:15, which says, "She is more precious than rubies: nothing you desire can compare with her." While that verse is in reference to wisdom, I believe God pulled out the isolated verse just for me. The other person came to me and said she saw a vision God told her was for me: It was of God with rubies in His hand, considering them as though they were precious to Him. Both of these words, I believe, were God's attempt to heal me right away from the arrows of Andrew's words. However, it was too close to the time I'd received the blow; I didn't let God's words sink into my heart. In fact, I hadn't even noticed the connection between rubies and a treasure until much later when I had gone back through my journals and realized what God tried to do for me.

At the end of my eight-month depression, I wanted all insecurities about my worth to be gone. I so desperately wanted to heal. Therefore, I reached out to the only One I knew could heal me of those wounds:

Jesus my Lord, my Divine Healer.

Around this time, I was taking Christian Leadership University's class called *Prayers that Heal the Heart*. One of the seven prayers for receiving inner healing is to pray for God to replace painful pictures with healing ones. The Virklers's book says, "The goal is to remove the sin energies attached to negative pictures which stem from traumatic events in your life by inviting Jesus to show you what He was doing in the situation and how His love and mercy and grace were there sustaining you." (3)

I needed to see what Jesus was doing during that painful scene, so I could finally heal. His words alone were not enough. I needed to replace a painful picture with a positive one. When I prayed for Jesus to heal this scene for me, what He did next touched my heart and restored me.

In reality, when this talk happened, Andrew and I were in my apartment sitting across two couches. In the reconstructed scene, where I believe the Holy Spirit moved and showed me what Jesus was doing, Jesus sat beside me, holding out those rubies in the palm of His hand. He was smiling at them, holding them out in front of me so the rubies were all I could see. Then, the verse came to me in Isaiah 49:15b-16a, "I will not forget you! See, I have engraved you on the palms of my hands."

Later in journaling with God about this scene, I felt like He said this to me:

(2004)

God: You accepted [Andrew's] words that you are not a treasure as a curse for future relationships. This must be broken. We can break it together. I have told you, you are a treasure. Your worth is not in another person and in his opinions of you. Your worth comes from Me. You can walk around with your head held high knowing what a treasure you are to your Heavenly Father. You no longer need to doubt. Do not accept that curse. You welcomed it into your heart and took it seriously. You questioned your worth and lovability based on the opinion of another human being. I am

here to break that for you. You can experience My healing,
My warm, loving healing to not let those words grow in your
heart any longer. That curse ends today. It is broken. It is
done. I have taken care of it. [Andrew] never meant it that
way, nor should you have taken it that way.

God's words and pictures delivered me from this pain. I want to call attention to the fact that even God said, in Andrew's defense, that Andrew didn't say those words to be cruel to me or to comment on my worth as a person. It's because of my history that I took it to heart; that is why it hurt me so badly and why it took me so long to heal. This was a man who just wanted to do the right thing in letting me go.

God's healing is so penetrating that it can wipe away pain, so much that I felt restored. I lost all sense of bitterness that I had built up against Andrew. To me, that alone felt like a miracle. I didn't think I'd ever get to a place where I felt peaceful about what happened with us. But when God heals, He does the job right; He does it thoroughly. I thought I'd want to avoid Andrew forever. Instead, God helped me face him again and restored the friendship for a short season, so I could see how healed I was! I can honestly say I am so thankful I had him in my life. The situation with him drove me into the love relationship I now treasure between God and me.

Exit the Wilderness God's Way

If you are in the wilderness, do you want to get out?

It took eight very long and dark months to walk through that depression. A couple of weeks after I received that inner healing picture, my depression started to lift. One day, I woke up and realized I was feeling better. I looked around at my life. Not one thing had changed. Not one circumstance, not one single hope had been fulfilled. I still didn't have someone to love. I still didn't have writing work. I was still just partially employed. Somehow, I had joy in my heart—God's joy passed on to me. I realized our attitudes shouldn't be dependent on what our lives look like. If our joy is dependent on anything but God, we may lose the source of that joy. Any other sources of joy can become idols before God. God is a jealous God who doesn't put up with idols. God wanted me to get to a place where all I had was Him, a place where I could honestly say to God, "You alone are enough." It took me a long time in the wilderness to get there.

Getting past your anxiety disorder may mean facing your biggest fear. Anything you clutch too tightly out of fear is likely to be taken away. God wants nothing between you and Him. He wants the number one slot in your life and won't take anything less. If comfort and safety are what you are clinging to, expect them to be challenged.

Say, for example, God asks you to open your heart to a new area of ministry involving public speaking, yet you fear public speaking like the plague. Fear is not a reason God excuses us from what He wants us to do. (Just ask Moses!) Doesn't God always ask us to move out of our comfort zones? For me, my comfort zone is writing and hiding behind the page, not reaching out and talking to people. That's when God says, "Go talk to people." He wants us dependent on Him and not on our own strength.

Following God guarantees we'll be standing out on a ledge, trusting He'll be there to catch us if we step over the edge. Cling to God, not a safety net, not what makes you feel secure, not circumstances, not a spouse or a job. Nothing!

The plain fact is that hardship, pain, and trials will always be in our lives. Each trial we survive makes us stronger, equips us to help others and makes us deeper people. God has the choice to not intervene, even when we beg Him to.

Are you still in the wilderness? Are you complaining about God not letting you out? If so, it's time to invite Him in and let Him show you the way out.

To Curse or Not to Curse

Is God really to blame if we suffer pain when we obey Him? I want to share one last thing that was instrumental in healing my relationship with God. When I wrestled with the idea of not wanting to follow God anymore because I felt He betrayed me, a trusted friend and counselor helped turn my thinking around. She first asked if I'm only willing to follow God if things turn out the way I want them to. I retorted that I never expected it to turn out badly. I also said I could have dealt with the bad if God had at least shown up to heal me. (I still believed He wasn't doing anything, and that made me so angry!) Then she pointed out that when we choose to follow God and obey Him, it is not God's fault when bad things happen to us. We have the freewill to follow or not to follow. Whatever happens after we say "yes" is not God's fault. I was thinking, *Excuse me? Are you kidding?* I stared at her blankly, rather annoyed. *How could it not be God's fault when I'm emotionally bleeding and crying and been in the dark for so long?*

Then she mentioned a perfect illustration: Jesus said "yes" to God's instruction for Him to come to earth, become human, then be crucified to save the world. What would it have been like if with every slash Jesus received, He cursed God, His Father, for letting something bad happen to Him? Jesus was obeying God. Should God have protected His Son from all that pain? No. Jesus was fulfilling God's divine purpose! Of course, the idea of Jesus cursing God for that pain sounds ridiculous. Jesus agreed to die so we could be saved; Jesus chose to walk divinely in God's will. So, why would He curse God for each ugly slur? Each slash? Each pierce? Each infliction of great pain? Jesus would never do that!

And neither should we, when we suffer pain.

We should never curse God, no matter what we have to endure, whether it's out of obedience to God or not. God doesn't only ask for our obedience; He asks for our surrender as well. That includes surrendering the way we hope a situation will turn out. We need to remember our fellow humans have that freewill stuff that allows them to choose in and outside God's will. Sometimes, that causes us much pain. I was abused as a kid because of someone's freewill. I am not alone in that. There's not a person in this world who hasn't been hurt by the free choice of someone else.

If I hadn't roughed out that year with God, I wouldn't have lived this chapter. This, as well as the Appendix of journal writings, serves as an example of where God acted as my Counselor through depression. I was 32 years old. And never in those 32 years had I imagined by that age I'd still be alone, still not have a family of my own, still not have love in my life.

But God's timing is perfect, even when it doesn't match mine.

Ways had to be paved first, growth had to happen. I have to take responsibility for slowing my progress down with my anger toward God.

God saved me; He loves me; He owes me nothing. Anything He does for me while I'm still on this earth is extra. It is not about our lives here; it's about our eternal souls and our love relationship with Him.

Where are you on your journey with God? Try to get to a point with God where you can honestly say, "Okay, God, You are enough for me. No matter what happens to me, no matter what I lose, no matter what pain I suffer, I will always love You. I will not blame You. My pain is not Your fault. My anxiety disorder is not Your fault. You are still my God, still Lord of my life, no matter what!"

That's what this journey is all about. Trusting God, surrendering to Him, and seeing the good in painful situations. I may not have wanted any of this pain. But I needed the pain so I could get where I was headed… my final destination. Peace.

I'll end this chapter on a poetic passage written by my friend, Chris Stacy, which I think speaks to all of our journeys:

Find your path and follow it. Walk. Don't run. A walking man sees the flowers and tastes the air around him. A running man sees only a flash of colors — the end of the path before it even begins. On this path, you will run into many obstacles: high walls, deep valleys, cold rivers. But you must remember the walls can only be so high and so wide. The valleys can only be so deep. The rivers can only be so cold. Take heart, if this is truly your path. The walls were made for you to climb, the valleys for you to cross, the rivers for you to wade through.

CHAPTER 12

The Destination:
Still Waters

The Lord is my shepherd; I shall not want. He maketh
me to lie down in green pastures; He leadeth me beside
the still waters.
(Psalm 23:1–2, kjv)

Over the years, I have ached to write this chapter; I longed for the completion of my story. The one that allowed me to prove I was no longer afraid of intimacy, which would also be the beginning of a whole new journey.

I finished penning the first draft of this book on Easter 2004. It was a wonderful resurrection weekend, a time when I felt my depression had fully lifted. I've added updates to prior chapters over the years (like my story of meeting the writer of the special *Webster* episode in 2007). But for the most part, this book has remained untouched. On a shelf. Collecting dust, along with me.

How could I finish this book without the end of my story?

It remained a matter of faith all of those years that I was healed of my panic disorder as it related to intimacy. I believed my fear of men was gone and that I'd finally be able to move into marriage and enjoy physical intimacy without having panic attacks.

Except I had no way to prove that theory.

There wasn't even anyone available to date, let alone marry. I was not about to enjoy intimacies that should be saved for marriage, just to prove my own healing. I'd waited long enough; I wanted to wait to give the gift of my virginity to my husband.

This unwritten chapter, "Chapter 12," has been the nickname of my "missing" husband for a long time, with many outcries to God asking, "Where is my Chapter 12?"

If you've read my book for singles, *Finally the Bride: Finding Hope While Waiting,* you know exactly what I'm talking about. I wrote *Finally Fearless* first, up through Chapter 11. *Finally the Bride* covered the many years of waiting that followed, as a single person, trying to keep hope alive in the midst of a long wait. I decided to release that book before this one.

The only anxiety I felt during the waiting years was that anxiousness to move on with life. I was not at all anxious to date anymore.

God's Promise

In the appendix of this book is a journal entry I'd like to include here as well, which was a promise God made to me in 2004, around the time I finished this book:

> God: My tender Cheryl, let me love you for a while. Make Me enough. Your love is coming. He is coming. Put it aside for now and wait on Me. You will watch My faithfulness unfold. You have plenty to focus on right now. It will sneak up on you when you least expect it. Lay it all down. I have given you plenty of tasks. Focus on those. Let Me pave the way for your love story. You don't need to do anything. Let Me write your love story. Let Me be the Author.

I took God up on that word. I gave Him the pen to my love life and waited on Him to author the story. (Maybe it wasn't that simple, and the whole experience warranted writing a whole separate book.)

Also in 2004, God encouraged me at a prayer meeting when a prophetic prayer warrior received a vision for me. She saw a picture of the stomach and bowel area and the area leading up to the heart. It was covered with a silver, protective lining. It had an opening at the top, like a balloon facing skyward. The woman said God revealed the meaning to her as my heart is protected, and no one can get in except the one God has for me. My job was to wait on God to give me the right person who's allowed into my heart and that person would be a gift from God. She was a little baffled by why this picture showed the protected stomach and bowel area. I understood this right away because of my anxiety issues. As you know, those were the areas where I was plagued most often with anxiety symptoms in any dating situation before. To know they were now protected was such a great comfort to the healing I would enjoy once I got married.

Knowing this and believing it only made me all the more impatient with desire for it. God's promises were both comforting and kicked up desire like wildfire.

I had this story I wanted to share with the world, to help others heal from panic disorders, as well as another book about God speaking through dreams. Both were shelved. I had this promise to come with no end in sight to the wait.

The main fear I battled in the next phase of my journey was manifested in questioning God. Sometimes I'd ask, "Did God really speak to me? Am I really just to sit here and wait on Him? Is He at work? Or am I just waiting for nothing?"

It was definitely a time of wrestling with God.

Some people who knew I wrote this book asked me why I wouldn't just release it before I got married. Why did I need to be married to prove I was healed? I always felt like I couldn't put a book out there claiming I was healed when I hadn't faced that final fear yet. It was a fear I knew could only be faced once I got married.

Could I release a book to say I had gotten over those fears of intimacy when I hadn't experienced it yet? I didn't think so.

In those seven plus years, I never officially dated anyone. I definitely had many friendships and encounters with guys, so much that I turned the "drama" of my single life into a comedy screenplay and novel called *Never the Bride*. I loosely based the story on my relationship with God and the theory that He had promised to write me a love story (from the journal entry I just shared). I even included our fights over how long He was taking.

Thankfully, I genuinely desired love and marriage the whole time. Not once did I want to shy away from finding them because of fear.

And then it happened.

A man pursued my heart.

Way Back When

In 1996, after Nathan and I stopped dating and I started counseling to "fix" this anxiety problem, I also began to go to my church's singles group in North Carolina. It was actually being a part of this group that caused me to feel like a social phobic, that feeling I journaled about earlier in this book. This was also the season of time when I journaled that I felt like such a "freak." This was the same church where I had to sit on the end of pews, not in the middle, so I wouldn't get claustrophobic and have to run out. This was the church I pictured when I penned the scene of Katie leaving her fiancé Danny at the altar in *Katie's Mountain*.

I hated going to this singles group; I made myself go because I knew I would never meet anyone, not even girls who were my own age, if I didn't start hanging out with others. Before grad school—where I met Nathan—I had been going to this church but working hard with the youth group and the kids on the drama programs. That left little time to meet friends, especially guys, my own age. Upon returning from grad school, I knew I had to change some things socially.

In grad school, I got used to having friends my age with similar interests. I hungered for that again once I graduated. It was way easier to make friends in film school than it was at a very large church's singles group. Our church had about 6000 members. You could easily disappear into the crowd if you didn't go to other events and get involved in groups. So, off to the singles group I went.

While it was a rather large group of singles, there was one guy who caught my attention.

His name was Chris Price.

My sister actually pointed him out to me, wishing I would go out with him. But I had it in the back of my mind that I was only going to be in North Carolina for a few years to save up for my big move to Los Angeles. I didn't want a guy holding me back. But truthfully, when you're in counseling over your fear of men, you're not all that interested in dating them anyway. Plus, Chris never asked me out.

He did, however, volunteer for me twice when I needed extras to be in two television shows I was producing. One was a teen detective series pilot, where he pretended to still be in high school for me. The other was a tax quiz show. (I even gave him a line on that show!)

Ironically, even though we didn't officially meet until 1996, Chris saw me for the first time in 1992, when I was directing the stage action of a Christmas pageant called *The Best Story Ever Told*. He remembers me kneeling down at the front of the stage, miming movements for the kids to follow. (I had choreographed some dance and sign language numbers and had to sit in front of them to remind the little four and five-year-olds what to do.) He remembers the real donkey I ordered to be in the show for Mary to use as she rode to the stable. (It was a high-class play.) The irony of its title being the first exposure Chris ever had to me is not lost on me.

The Best Story Ever Told.

Most people who hear our love story believe it's one of the best love stories they've ever heard.

Remember my story about writing myself a boyfriend (to be played by Kirk) into a skit for a contest back in 1986? That skit contest was held in the gym of this same church location. As a fourteen-year-old, I had no idea I'd meet this special guy there one day or that he'd be playing music gigs on this same stage I acted on.

My last memory of Chris before my aforementioned move to Los Angeles was crossing paths with him and a girl in the balcony at church. He had his hand gently placed on her back as he guided her through the walkway to find a seat. He and I smiled at each other and said hello. Inside, I thought, "Oh well, I guess he found someone. I'm moving away anyway." There was that small pang, but I brushed it off.

I moved away in 2000 and never saw him again for ten years.

Not until he showed up on Facebook as a friend of a mutual friend.

And little did I know, "way back when," that one day, the "only cute guy in the singles group" would play such a significant role in my future.

Reconnection

It was March 2010 when I was wasting time on Facebook. (Not unusual for me.) I saw an old friend: Chris Price. Guitar in hand, he was playing music in his photo. He was still in North Carolina. There was no relationship status listed, but a quick scroll through his pictures seemed to indicate he was still single and without a family of his own.

Despite my "trolling" (or Face-Stalking as my friends and I like to call it), I was interested in someone else. I sent Chris a friend request anyway. Why not? I thought it would be fun to say hello to a long-lost friend. I wasn't even sure he'd remember me. He did.

In fact, just three days earlier, he had thought about me after ten years of not thinking about me. (I tried not to be offended about that fact. I can't say I thought much about him either.)

So, to Chris, my reaching out to him over Facebook was more than significant. In fact, he thought it might have God written all over it! From the very beginning, my reemergence into his life felt like God may be putting us together.

Because of my interest in someone else at the time (one of those friends I hoped would "wake up" to my irresistible charms), I wasn't very easy on Chris. I was honest about my interest in someone else, and I actually said no to considering a relationship with him for about six months.

A New Relationship; A New Battle

Chris was direct; he was a real pursuer.

In some ways, that made me nervous. For the past seven years, I had liked various guys. None of them liked me in return. That made them somewhat safe. (There's a high emotional risk, liking someone who has virtually no chance of liking you back, but no physical risks.)

With Chris, for the first time, I had someone clearly pursuing me. We had a lot of deep conversations during those six months prior to our first date. Before I flew to North Carolina for Thanksgiving (to visit him and my family), I knew he had a lot riding on it. I could sense from his conversations that he truly suspected that I was his future wife. I, however, was not ready to say anything so definitive.

I'll admit that, shortly before that trip, I started to get nervous about it. I experienced some anxiety symptoms but nothing close to a panic attack. I tried to separate out what were normal, first date jitters versus what were abnormal and part of my disorder. Sometimes, it was hard to tell, and I could feel myself "overreacting" to an obviously safe situation.

A mentor told me how she hadn't seen me that nervous in a while, and she felt like Satan was trying to steal my healing, or trying to convince me that I wouldn't be okay. You know how easy those thought processes can send us down the wrong road, and we can even bring on panic attacks if we let our thoughts take us too far.

It suddenly dawned on me: I knew I was healed. I was not about to let Satan rob me of that. I had to fight back, but I didn't want to fight back alone. I wanted to enlist the prayers of my trusted mentors.

To follow is a journal entry I wrote shortly before Chris and I spent time together in person:

> *Cheryl's Journal (November 2010)*
>
> *I'm praying Chris will have a calming effect on me. Let that be a signal to me that I'm safe. If he does, maybe I'll feel safe enough to open my heart and know he'll stay with me. It's important to my anxiety ministry that I not panic over him. That can't be my story. Not just because it shouldn't be, but I honestly feel like it's not supposed to be a problem, and I'm succumbing to a blatant attack of the enemy trying to derail me. The game changed; the battle changed. Because I may be so close to what God has for me, the devil wants to take me down. I have my marching orders from God. Satan will not take me down. This is the first time a man is actually pursuing me in this way, and I have to realize: this is a good pursuit, and his attention is good. It's not the bad kind of attention from long ago. It's also not the frustrating kind that other guy friends have given me that's been ambiguous about if they want a relationship with me or not. I'm safer with Chris than I was with any of those guys, but that may be why I've been anxious. This is real and could be it. My "finally" that I've been waiting for. I think I'm realizing how real this all may be and how the enemy can't win this battle over me. I'm close to a victory.*

My first plan of attack—even though Chris didn't know my life story yet—was to share my need for prayer warriors with him (and a little bit about why) so he could be lifting me up. I wanted to give him a chance to battle in prayer because he'd already proven to be quite a prayer warrior about other things. Immediately, he was on task in warfare on my behalf.

Suddenly, I wasn't facing this alone. Someone had my back, one I suspected could be my gift from God. I was able to calm down and even look forward to us finally spending time together. He proved to me that he cared about me—challenges and all—right from the beginning. I want to share an email he sent me when I shared with him my need for prayer over my fears:

> *Cheryl,*
>
> *Thank you so much for sharing with me and for trusting me enough to put that out there for me. Also, HECK YES I will be praying for you. I have been but know better how to target my prayers now. Actually, the pastor at this conference I was at today said, "How many of you want a victory?" And everyone raised their hands. Then he said, "Well, there's no victory without a battle." And that's just the way it is. However, we have the victory in Jesus already. He already did everything for us that we will ever need on the cross. His job is finished. Ours isn't. But we do our job now based on what He's already done. I agree with your mentor that this is totally a spiritual thing, and the timing of it is not a coincidence. I'm not just talking about us, but I'm also referring to all the open doors the Lord is bringing your way.*
>
> *The enemy sees what the Lord has in store for you, and there's no way he's going to let it happen without a fight and probably a hard one. He knows the influence that entertainment and movies have on people, and he doesn't want yours to get made because they will impact thousands and millions of people for the Kingdom of God. Not only does the enemy want to stop your ministry, but he also wants to destroy you. However, I have great news to remind you of. You belong to God. You are His property, bought and paid for. You have a destiny and a purpose to fulfill here on earth that only you can do. The Lord has really good plans for you and your life. You are not alone. You have friends,*

family, and now me, fighting this with you and helping you to stand. God gives us authority in Jesus' Name over the enemy and everything that would oppose the Kingdom of God. Your part: you need to rebuke the enemy in Jesus' Name, fill your heart and mind with what Jesus says about you in His Word, make your thoughts and feelings submit to and line up to the Word of God. You need to speak encouragement over yourself and speak God's promises over you – out loud – with your mouth. If you have your prayer language you need to pray like crazy in the Spirit and trust the Lord to bring you through this. Remember, you are more than a conqueror in Him, not a scraper-byer. Our part (your friends and family) is to cover you with our prayers and to lift you up to the Lord constantly. To break this spirit off of you and to bind it and cast it down in Jesus' Name. To stand in the gap for you and to fight for you and with you. To fast and pray for you.

I personally sense that you are on the threshold of a mighty victory, Cheryl, and I'm excited to participate with you in obtaining it. Well, have a great night and I pray the Lord's peace over you tonight, keeping your heart and your mind stayed on Him. May He refresh you and draw you closer to Him. Sleep well. Now, if you'll excuse me, I need to go to WAR!

The Victory is yours,
Chris

Chris almost won me over with this note alone. It felt so good to have someone there to lean on, who understood this was a spiritual battle, waged by an enemy who wanted to convince me that God had never healed me. Once I saw the battle for what it was, I was able to calm down.

After I got his note, I wrote the following in my journal:

Cheryl's Journal (November 2010)

His note shows me so much of who he is. If Chris can handle the most difficult parts of me without having seen the good parts (and he's still sticking around) then I have a keeper. I love that he wrote I'm on the threshold of victory. That is beyond true, God, if he is indeed your intended for me. It also brings the long-awaited conclusions to three books. It brings completion to my testimony with Never the Bride. *It would give me my anxiety victory, my marriage, and family. This is all on you, God, to get me there.*

Celebrating Victories

After six months of communicating from opposite coasts, I was able to spend two weeks with Chris without having any anxiety problems. I had a bit of those first date jitters, but only to what's normal to most of the human race. It was nowhere near close to panic attacks. I felt safe enough to share many meals with him, without a single embarrassing incident.

Our first official date, incidentally, was a sixteen-hour trip to the mountains of North Carolina and back. One of our stops was Bridal Veil Falls, one of the shooting locations for *The Hunger Games*. (No, that place and its name wasn't awkward or anything!) We took our picture in front of the sign. Prophetic perhaps?

During that trip, I shared my life story with him. I'll admit: it was a bit awkward. It was hard to dive into something so serious so soon. However, I didn't want my past issues to have any power over me. I didn't want to "hide." I figured if he cared about me, he'd be able to handle it. I had told him in advance that I wanted to share that story with him that day, to hold myself accountable. I didn't want to chicken out, just because it felt uncomfortable.

We'd had enough deep conversations before our first date that it wasn't like a normal first date. In hindsight, I might have waited at least a couple of dates in until we had bonded a little more. Those first, in-person encounters weren't our favorites. It took a while to warm up to being together in person, which is a vastly different vibe than email and Facebook conversations. It might have made the serious conversation a little easier.

Regardless, I was met with a listening ear and kind-hearted understanding from Chris. Even with the highest risk of all being so close to my fingertips—knowing he just might be "the one"—I had no panic issues at all.

Close Encounters

Chris seemed to have excellent instincts about physical intimacy and never pushed the envelope on boundaries. Our last day together of my first trip to see him, we took a trip down to Charleston, South Carolina to scout locations for my film, *Never the Bride*. It's such a romantic and beautiful city. As we walked under the Folly Beach Pier, Chris took my hand in his. It was a sweet moment. I wasn't ready to say yet that we were going to end up together, but it was nice to enjoy his affection without panicking.

On my second trip, just weeks later, for Christmas, we took another excursion to the mountains. This time, we went to the Biltmore House in Asheville, North Carolina. (Thankfully, this didn't take sixteen hours.) On the stunning property, in a gazebo overlooking the mountains at sunset, we enjoyed our first kiss. We both sensed this would be our "last first kiss." It was wonderful to enjoy appropriate physical contact without any anxiety problems. It was such a joy to finally experience even a slice of my healing. (I won't mention that my mother called in the middle of this first kiss session to find out what I wanted for lunch the next day.)

By the end of my second North Carolina trip in December, we knew we had something very good and real. In January, we acknowledged that we knew we were going to get married. Chris flew out to Los Angeles to visit me the week of Valentines Day 2011. (Yes, Valentines Day was finally redeemed for me. It wasn't about gifts: it was our celebration together that we finally had love and a person worth celebrating!) There was such safety, knowing he loved me. I was able to give my heart permission to fall in love again.

On the Santa Monica Pier, on February 18, 2011 (our three-month anniversary), we got engaged. Let me explain how redeeming this was. Remember my biggest heartbreak with Andrew? Andrew and I spent our three-month anniversary on this same beach, the big date that was just days after he told me I should start guarding my heart with him. Even my most horrible break up with Andrew was on this very same beach, less than a month later. It was this same place in January 2004, when I was at a crossroads, trying to decide if I still wanted to serve and follow God, after all the pain He had allowed. That desperate prayer I journaled on the beach was in this place.

Interestingly, while my relationship with Andrew ended during its fourth month, with Chris, we got to start planning our wedding during its fourth month.

Having Chris propose at this most beautiful, amazing location, one that had originally held such painful memories, was so redeeming. He used purple M&Ms to propose to me, which included phrases like "I want you" and "I choose you." Remember how much I felt unchosen and untreasured? All that pain was wiped away.

I had no idea that painful day in the summer of 2003, that one day, the right guy would come along and propose to me in the same place. Chris didn't even know he was doing this; he just knew it was one of my favorite places in Los Angeles. (It sure made for a gorgeous place for engagement photos! In fact, the picture on the cover of this book— those two love birds running toward the ocean, looking so free—that is one of our photos on the Santa Monica beach from the day we got engaged.)

Facing the Intimacy to Come

I knew being engaged meant marital intimacy would follow. I'll admit: a few of those fears started to creep up again. I had some fear of pain and knew that I didn't want to associate my husband with pain. I wanted clean memories and no chance of having flashes to my past abuse.

During that time, I went on a search for a book to help an abuse survivor thrive in intimacy. I didn't need to read another book on healing from abuse; I had already read many of those. I'm talking about one that takes the journey to that next, positive level.

I couldn't find such a book, especially not one written from a biblical perspective.

In talking to a few close friends and mentors about the type of book I wished I could read, four of them told me one day I'd probably be writing that book. Since no book seemed to exist, I went on a journey with God and asked Him to counsel me in advance of my wedding day and honeymoon. My husband and I will include that part of our story in another book to come about growing marital intimacy, as it's too much to contain within what's left of this chapter. I will say God counseled me a lot from January 2011, all the way through to my wedding day and honeymoon. He held my hand through this monumental transition in life from a single virgin, formerly fearful woman to a loving, fearless, affectionate, and intimate wife.

We got married on May 14, 2011. The day was a victorious turning point for me.

My grandmother, who had struggled with anxiety of her own, was still alive when I penned this book up through Chapter 11. I had always wanted her to be at my wedding, to see me finally be victorious over all of my fears. However, she died in January 2010. At that time, I inherited her engagement ring, the one she faithfully wore until the day she died, even though my grandfather had passed in the sixties. I knew I wanted this to be my engagement ring; it was a meaningful way to allow her to share in my special day.

Before my wedding, I often thought of the original story I penned about my anxiety disorder, *Katie's Mountain*, where the girl leaves her future husband at the altar because she's too afraid to go on their honeymoon. (They hadn't been intimate sexually yet).

The morning of my wedding, while I had normal bride jitters knowing I was about to walk into a room where over 100 people would be watching me, nothing in me wanted to run. Well, except maybe the instinct to run *to* the altar to get to my man quicker, like my character in *Never the Bride* does! Only a sprained ankle the week of the wedding prevented that. Plus, it gave me the joy of letting my father walk me down the aisle.

From a Healed Place

I'm so happy to say that I was right about my healing. God did such a thorough work that I had no trouble being intimate with my husband throughout our whole honeymoon, from the first time onward. I did not need anti-anxiety meds to make it through a single intimate moment, including the first time. (I had them with me just in case I needed some extra help, but I found I didn't need them.)

In our private times, my past history was nowhere near my thoughts. I was able to be with Chris and not see sexual interest as distorted or something to fear. It's like God gave me the grace to forget the past during times of intimacy. Only later would I get the chance to reflect how my history had no impact on my enjoyment of our sex life.

God gave me an amazing husband who was sensitive to my need for safety. He is the most tender, caring, and loving husband I ever could have asked for. We feel like God showed up in the midst of it all to celebrate with us, our one-flesh union as husband and wife. (After all, sex and becoming one was God's idea.)

I can honestly testify now to my complete and total healing and say the fears are truly gone. I praise God for His thorough work in me, and for showing me that anxiety, fear, and panic can be overcome.

Now, having just hit our one-year anniversary, I continue to testify the same. Fear has never entered our bedroom. So I'm happy to be a witness that healing can take place.

If you want to read more about our love story (and especially if you are single and waiting), I encourage you to read our other book, *Finally the Bride*. It covers a whole different side of our dynamic and God-written love story, as well as what to do as a single while waiting.

I was able to fulfill my dream of having Chris co-write with me through that book instead of this one, since we decided to release that one first. He shares his side of our story there.

No matter what you are afraid of, no matter what you panic over, God can offer healing. It may take a long time; God is not an instant God in many cases. It takes work. The work is well worth it, especially when it allows you to move into all that God has for you to enjoy, no longer held by the bars of fear.

I pray for you on your journey that God will meet you where you are, and then lead you someplace new: a place where fear no longer rules your life and decisions.

Trust God to lead you, even if at first it seems like He's taking you into some painful places. There is no safer place to be than in God's healing hands and walking down that path to the right side, even if at first it's dark and seems a little scary. If you don't, you could be missing out on *living* your life.

May God and His grace be with you as you journey toward those still waters called peace.

APPENDICES

A. My Prayer Journaling and Dialoguing with God

B. 12-Step Method

APPENDIX A

My Prayer Journaling and
Dialoguing With God

To follow are select journal entries from 2003–2004. It's a mix of my prayers to God before, during, and after the most challenging relationship I've ever had, as well as some of God's answers. I was able to hear God clearly after the relationship ended, when God wanted to heal my depression. I strongly encourage you to read Chapter 11 first; it sets the background for what I was going through during this time.

January 12, 2003:

The Book of Job shows a man of God, who, in his humanness, cried out in pain when his good life took a bad turn. He doesn't blame God, just requests that God take his pain away or kill him. It's a book with lots of complaining; perhaps that's why he's one of the easiest characters to relate to. We all question our existence, why we're here, especially when we're hurting. I especially relate to Job being met with silence by God, which I don't understand. I guess it's part of the test to prove Job wouldn't curse God, regardless of whether God spoke. But why is God a God who sits back and watches our suffering and chooses silence for a season?

January 20, 2003:

Last night, God told me to give Andrew another chance. It would be scary, of course, and challenging to ever try again. But I feel it's important to allow God to work. It would require a lot of faith. This risk would be so monumental to me.

January 22, 2003:

Lord, if You want Andrew and me to be the vessels who help each other, I'm open to it. But You need to make it very clear to me, and I would need You to walk with me every step of the frightening way. I'd never choose this on my own! But I believe, Lord, You can help both of us work through our issues. I'm sure these thoughts have something to do with why I haven't felt calm all day; I'm nervous. I can't even believe I'm entertaining such thoughts, even with some hope. The chances of this working are so slim! Lord, I can handle small amounts of anxiousness. That's normal. I feel beyond normal anxiety, yet no panics. Please help me keep it that way.

January 23, 2003:

Help me, Lord, to not make a mistake. If You want me in this, You must help me. My anxieties will need to go away because I will not enter a situation where I'll need drugs or feel insane. Will my being able to do this be a miraculous healing story? Because if ever I had grounds to be afraid, it would be in this relationship. *Please slam this door, Lord, if this will end extremely badly, with me getting hurt. I don't want this to blow up on me.*

February 12, 2003:

Last night, it happened. Andrew and I made the decision to try dating again. I sit here fighting anxiety and not wanting to eat. I need to get better. I hope I can use coping methods. I want God to continue to help me. I made it through an amazing change in our relationship without a single attack.

February 14, 2003:

Wow! I feel like I'm giving myself permission to feel. I am letting my walls go, and it doesn't feel scary. It feels like he is the one I will marry. I know it would be highly painful if it doesn't go there, and I haven't put up my protective walls. But anxiety has always been my defense, and I can't let that in. Thank You, Lord, for helping me break down the walls in the face of such risk. This feels nothing short of a miracle. This feels so orchestrated by You.

February 18, 2003:

I ask You for the blessing on my Panic book. I feel this is the season for me to work on it. A season of victory. A season where I have been able to put into practice what I've learned.

March 01, 2003:

Lord, the way You've systematically answered prayers, and answered my concerns makes me feel like this relationship is safe. The idea that I'm not guarding myself is just wild to me! But You've given me amazing peace. I'd be quite devastated if it didn't work.

March 17, 2003:

I feel like this will work. I was touched by Andrew's reaction to my script, *Katie's Mountain*, because it's obvious he cares. I feel so good about this relationship and hope it works out. I've never been this comfortable. No one's ever made the effort to get to know me the way he has.

April 11, 2003:

Why is my throat tight? Please, Lord, keep me calm. If I'm not calm, I'm not fun. Please let me rest in Your calm. I don't want Andrew to feel he's always paying for the part of him that makes me feel insecure. I don't want to tell him every time I get nervous. I want him to know I trust and believe in him. How much assurance am I allowed to ask for? Even though it's hard, nothing in me wants to run from this.

April 26, 2003:

Lord, I need You. I am incapable of doing this without You. I'm depending on You and need Your help.

May 06, 2003:

Last night's talk stripped me of any confidence and security I had in this relationship. Now he warns me to guard my heart. Well, it's a little late for that. I already love him. How am I supposed to stay in this relationship? With my security compromised, I won't be as fun, as warm. I won't be the person he's used to. How is he supposed to fall in love with a version of me he won't like because I'll be different? Guarded, protected, anxious. How am I supposed to live under that pressure? To attempt to stay normal without anxiety? I don't know how to exist this way. I feel like I'm back where I always end up: not chosen, not a treasure. This could be a set back for me in my own healing. I should just run away now.

May 12, 2003:

Last night, when we celebrated our anniversary, Andrew made amazing gestures to make me feel comfortable again. I don't want to run away now. That's what I've done my whole life. I want to stay and be brave. But God, You've got to help me! He is precious to me, Lord, and I don't want to face losing him. I want this to work. You've allowed me to open my heart for the first time ever. Please help it not backfire on me.

May 22, 2003:

It's weird. I keep having these dreams about Andrew. In them, he's always leaving, wanting space, wanting to take off alone, or he's nowhere to be found. Are these my abandonment issues shining through? I had three dreams with the same message in one night, waking up after each one.

May 26, 2003:

Okay, Lord. Here we are in Florida with my family. Things appear to be great. My family adores Andrew; he gets along with them. So, why is it, last night, I had five more dreams about Andrew leaving me?

Again, he was always walking the other way from me, escaping, running. I hated those feelings when I woke up. Are you trying to tell me something or am I being paranoid?

June 01, 2003:

My pain over never being chosen or loved by a man my entire life is a pain God knows exponentially. He feels this every time someone says no to Him. So, God certainly understands my pain. God understands us so much more than we can grasp. It resonated with me, watching the movie *Bruce Almighty*, when Jim Carrey asks Morgan Freeman's version of God about how you make someone love you when you can't mess with anyone's freewill. And God answered, "Welcome to my world." So true.

June 02, 2003:

Tonight at the Bible study, my friend had a word of prophecy for me. A preparation from God that this relationship will end. I guess God has been trying to warn me through dreams. I'm in awe the God of the universe has stepped out to talk to me this way. I'm in too much shock over the news to react. I'm thankful God also supplied some amazing promises to me about my future, something I can hold onto because I know I'm about to go through something awful.

June 09, 2003:

This is by far the most painful break I've ever experienced. Thank You, God, for the advance warning. My question for you, Lord, is why did You lead me into this relationship? I specifically asked You not to if it would just blow up in my face. I looked it up. January 23, 2003. Do I not get a say here? Does my will not matter? This just kills me! He walks away fine, ready to move on, and I'm emotionally shattered. Why do I ever let myself hope? As to my healing, I don't feel better. I wouldn't have lost so much weight if I were better. If I need someone's acceptance and unconditional love to not struggle with anxiety, then I can offer little to help others heal. I am not writing my book. I'm throwing it away. What's the point of it anyway? Lord, I have suffered for twenty years with anxiety and guys. Shouldn't that be enough?

June 22, 2003:

God, Your presence in my life is undeniable. I know You're here. I know You've been involved. I know You drew me to Andrew. What I need from You are some answers, some ways of understanding why this happened. Why was I lured into this? Why did I feel security, Your hand on the relationship? Couldn't You have given me less peace so I could have guarded my heart? Whose purpose was served for me to end up in this much pain, disappointment, and shattered hopes? I gasped, "Are You crazy?" when You asked me to give Andrew another chance. Why couldn't we have left it at that? Why would You want this for me? I am Your hurt child pleading before You from a very confused place. Even if this is a case where Andrew stepped out of Your will, You always knew he would. You knew ahead of time the pain I would suffer. Can You please meet me where I am and bring understanding into this situation? Why did You use me in a way that attacks my healing? I walked into the scariest risk of my life because You told me to! I don't get why this was for my good. I ended up with the broken heart, having lost one of the best friends I've ever had in my life. All I see here are major losses. No benefits. And it came out of my obedience to You.

June 25, 2003:

I want this all to be over. Life. I'm so tired of trying to do so many things that go nowhere. Dead ends. Dashed hopes. Why do I always let myself hope? Nothing has ever worked out. I'm miserable. Please, dear God, hear my cry. It's not supposed to be like this.

June 30, 2003:

[My friend] didn't know I've been suicidal and speaking my

stupid thoughts. But tonight, she gave me a word from God—I am to stop saying I want to disappear from this earth. I guess You really do hear my prayers, huh?

July 12, 2003:

Last night was such a dark night where I wished I could die and saw no point to my existence in this world. I can't believe how little there is to live for. I wonder when life's meaning will surface. Will I ever know why I needed to be here? Do I need to be here or is purpose just a figment of our manufactured, earthly hopes and imaginations? I don't know how not to hate life. I hate the depression, the suicidal thoughts, the surmounting problems. Losing a love, problems my family is having, being unemployed with no job prospects, having my writing and talent attacked by others, having my two best friends here say they're moving. All at the same time! How much more will I have to take? What else will pile up? Do I want to be here tomorrow to find out? Not really. My heart is ripped to shreds and others are kicking me while I'm down. It's insanity. I can't take much more. When will the sun come out again in my life? Lord, it's disappointing to be so far from the life I want.

July 24, 2003:

I need to accept that I am normal to still be in mourning over this. It's only been six weeks. It's healthier to deal with it now, instead of numbing myself, only to bring baggage into another relationship. I wish thoughts of me just disappearing would cease. I know, Lord, You've asked for better of me. I ask You to bring a miraculous healing to me. Can You help me understand if I'm doing anything to slow down my healing?

August 24, 2003:

Lord Jesus, Keeper of my soul, Counselor, the One who loves me deeper and more than any human could. This year started out with such promise with signs of a big turnaround in my life. And now, as it's almost September, it's become one of the worst, most painful years of my life. Is this the point I stop and wait on You for Your divine direction? I love and adore You and am thankful to be Your child. I can't imagine going through all of this without You. But I'm so lost as to what's going on with my life and why and what I'm supposed to do next. Lord, I ache to hear from You. Let me receive Your wisdom and guidance. Lead me, Lord. Directly. Through dreams. Through Your Word.

(After I wrote that entry, I tried to go to sleep. But I kept feeling like God was nudging me to get back up and start writing down what He wanted to say to me.)

God's reply: The blessings to come are tailored for you. Suited. Less challenging. You are healing. It was necessary for your growth. Not just (Andrew's). It was for you, too. The bitterness will fade and you will have understanding. You were a vessel. You learned, you grew, you depended on Me. I am not letting you down. You are prepared now to love. You were never willing to risk before. With pain comes understanding, depth. It mattered that you were in his life. It mattered that he was in yours. I used you and you were an open vessel. And yes, it caused you pain. I did not mislead you. You were where you needed to be. You did the right thing with honesty and truth. You loved freely, rightly, unselfishly. I ache with you in your pain. Know that I haven't missed an ounce of it. I've cried with you. I know it hurt. I led you in, and I led you out. Trust me — it was for your ultimate good. This helps you release bitterness. This is only a season. I am with you. I see your heart, your desire for Me and communication. Don't doubt My words. My presence. My gifts. I am with you. The darkness will fade. Hold on to the truthfulness of My words. I'm giving you understanding so you can heal and so you can hope. This is your year of growth. It's wise you've clung to Me despite difficulties. You've cried out in honesty. You've remained My child in all of this.

(Several of those words were then repeated by a friend who also hears God's voice. I hadn't shared these words with her. God confirmed the same truths to train me to recognize His voice.)

August 28, 2003:

Lord, my relationship with Andrew is where I chose to trust You. I had to trust You more than I ever had to in my entire life. What faith it took for me to walk into that! No wonder my relationship with You grew monumentally. You got my attention and communication out of this. I gained more depth and life experience, maturity and unselfishness. I learned how to love unconditionally through it. Giving more than taking. Offering grace and patience, caring about another's needs over mine. I guess that's something to be thankful for.

September 07, 2003:

Lord, I feel like last night you told me it won't be this year. That 2003 will not be the year I will know who my husband will be. This is so depressing. Can you please fill the void? Please tell me I heard you wrong. I cry because I will be 32 in just a few months. I never imagined I'd be this age and still alone.

September 8, 2003:

Cheryl's prayer: I feel like I'm chasing an uncatchable, unreachable wind. I ache tonight. I'm angered by Andrew's capacity to still hurt me. God, if you've told me I'm healing, why am I still crying? Today marks three months. Guess that's not too long. But I thought I made progress. God, it still hurts. I will never understand why You answer some people's prayers and not others.

God's reply: I am sovereign. I assign the breaths of your days. Years of your life. No, I don't make the same decisions for each person. But the essence of My character is unchanging. I am the same yesterday, today, and forever. I know what you've been through. You need to give Me a chance to do a work in you. Do not be discouraged. I know it hurts. The rejection. Just don't lose faith. Your heart is precious and will be taken care of. A crown of glory awaits. Just wait. I deliver on promises. All of them. Stand on them.

Cheryl's prayer: God, You know it hurts to be in love with You, too. This is so hard.

God's reply: My presence will become known to you more and more. Didn't I promise that I have a purpose for your life? Why, My daughter, are you so discouraged? I deal with each person individually. You needed a healing and that journey was part of your healing. You are walking the right road. There are so many roads for you and all are good. Stay in tune. Listen for Me. Keep loving Me. Keep praying to Me. Your suffering is not for nothing. I am preparing you. Deepening you. Refining you. You have grown so much this year and clung to Me. It's been beautiful. Stop saying it's your worst year because I see it as your best. A time you've cared most about Me and been willing to cast aside your agenda for Mine.

September 16, 2003:

(While God had just said some beautiful things to me a week earlier, I wasn't letting it sink in. I was still wallowing in depression:)

I like my imaginary world much better. I'm tired of trying so hard to make this happen, my personal and professional dreams. I'm tired of being so unhappy. I have nothing to offer this world or anything in it. If You don't care what's going on in my life, Lord, why should I care anymore? Why should I try?

Just take me from this miserable existence. Or can You change it? You keep promising to. Why am I even trying to affect the world through words? Nothing is working. Not writing. Not relationships. Can't my life have just one thing?

September 19, 2003:

> Lord, help me.
> Be with me.
> Comfort me.
> Most of the time I'd rather be dead.
> Help.
> What is the point of my life?
> Why am I here?

September 20, 2003:

Cheryl's prayer: How did this depression get such a stronghold on me, where I think of suicide and wishing I were dead all the time? I consider not eating so I can disappear. Why does life hold so much pain and misery? I don't know how to trust You. I don't know how to stop crying or pretend I don't feel how I feel. God, for me to shake a knife and ask You if I should plummet it into my wrist... how much lower can I possibly go? I feel anger brewing inside me. Where is my mind that I'm having these feelings? What is wrong with me? It's like something else has taken a hold of me and my mind.

God's reply: Don't you know that I love you and have your best interests at heart? You grieve. We all grieve. I grieve daily every person who says no to me. I grieve with My children who are in pain. I see your pain. I understand it; I've felt it. Draw near to Me; don't push Me away. Your life is precious. You're being molded. I never promised to make sense. Nor do I need to. You should trust Me. You don't trust Me with your heart.

Cheryl's prayer: It's hard to, Lord, when You are the one who told me to open it to Andrew, and it's caused me the most pain I've ever felt. I didn't know that would be a place You'd want to lead me. Even if You try to explain, it doesn't remove my pain, nor have You healed that pain. I can't believe how much it still hurts. I guess the human side of me wants You to fix the mess You got me into by asking me to obey You.

God's reply: You are My bride first and foremost. You are loved, even when you can't see it or feel it. You focus on the pain. I focus on your beauty, the strength of your heart capable of love, a love so pure. Persevere to the finish. There is a cloud lifting, but you are letting it defeat you. You forget that after the dark clouds move there is pure blue sky with a sun so bright. Do you want a gift before it's wrapped? Before it's paid for? You are My daughter. I delight in you, even when you don't delight in Me, even when you are angry. Cry out to Me. It's what you're supposed to do with your pain. It's better than drowning yourself with substances that will not change your life. You are wise to come to Me, even in your anger. Do not rebel. I see your pain. I can take your pain. Let Me have it. It can belong to Me now so you can rest. You need rest. You work and work, but it's time for rest. Let your heart rest and breathe. I can breathe life back into it. I am the Restorer.

September 23, 2003:

Jesus, if You have anything to do with some of this depression lifting, I thank You. Maybe You're answering the prayers of my amazing friends who've been praying for me. At least for today, I don't want to die. I wish I weren't swayed so much by life's circumstances. I welcome You to change my life, take it and change it in the right ways.

October 1, 2003:

I can't believe we're in the last quarter of the year. What do I have to show for it? Why is the joy of friends so painful to me? I want You, the same God who gave and delivered promises to my friends, to deliver on promises to me. But with my attitude, why would You? I've become someone I can barely stand to be with. It makes me want to stay away from others so they don't have to be exposed to my ugliness. God, where are You in my life?

October 12, 2003:

God, I know we're not on the best terms right now. I am filled with hurt and anger, as though I've been done wrong. Maybe it's time I shut up and listen to what You have to say for once. I fear damage that can be done the longer we stay off track.

October 19, 2003:

Lord, please bring my husband to me. I'm ready to write Chapter 12, the end of my success story. Open his eyes to me, my eyes to him.

October 24, 2003:

Lord, have I missed something You'd like me to do? Is there anything I've been disobedient to? Please direct me as I'm open to You. I know Your definition of success is completely different from mine. I get that. I don't want to get in Your way. Lord, enrich my life with Yourself, and restore my heart.

(Shortly after this, God confirmed for me that He wanted me to take classes in Christian Counseling at Christian Leadership University. This was to help me heal and for the purpose of drafting this book.)

Lord, I feel drawn to taking classes because it will bring me closer to You and help me learn what I need to learn to finish this book. It will help me discern Your voice. I want my book to be full of You and Your wisdom, not mine.

November 03, 2003:

Lord, thank You for working out my healing. And thank You for helping me work on my book outline. It feels more important than any script I could write. I know You're healing me. I know You have a ministry for me, even if it takes me light-years away from my comfort zone.

November 09, 2003:

Cheryl's prayer: Lord, is there anything you want to say to me today?

God's reply: My Word does not return to Me void. The words I speak come to pass, come to fruition. This includes the words and promises I've spoken directly into Your life. I've spoken often, and You have heard Me. You will continue to hear Me. I will speak in many forms, many ways. I am not limited to one method. Keep watch and see what I will do with your life. You are My precious child. I will honor you for your obedience, the doors you've walked through without knowing why. I see your faith and love for Me. I love you, My child. Your life is changing. A living water will come forth to others through you and your ministries. You will be used by Me, and I will be with you. I am beside you, not behind or ahead. I will bless you for investing time in Me and our relationship. You do not walk alone. And you will not always be alone in this earthly presence either. I am preparing one, and he is amazing for you. He also loves Me. He will love and cherish you in a way that wipes away evils, past hurts. Not to worry, my daughter, your heart is taken care of. I've heard your cry, your anguish. I'm preparing the one for you. He is a gift from Me.

December 28, 2003:

Cheryl's prayer: Lord, how do I get to that point in this wilderness where it no longer hurts me to have all those voids? When will I say, "Okay, God, do what you will, even if it doesn't come close to what I want"? I don't want to be looking for the right job or the right person to make me happy. How do I live with these voids and feel joy anyway? How do I truly make You my joy, my all?

God's reply: Reach out to Me. When You are experiencing pain and tears, it does not mean you displease Me. You are still Mine. A lot of My people experienced depression. You are not alone. Cling and hold tight; don't push away. Rest in My shadow. You are My child, no matter how you feel or act. There is a way for you to experience joy despite circumstances. It's through having faith in Me, trusting in Me and understanding that My timing is perfect and right. As you surrender to Me and don't work against Me, I can move and work.

January 18, 2004:

Cheryl's prayer: Lord, You possibly instruct me not to take meds. Yet, then I want to drink a whole bottle of codeine cough syrup to feel better. I don't exactly desire to be on meds, but I don't want to keep feeling this way either. I don't want to talk to anyone who knows me. I don't want people to see me this way. What used to interest me before I can't stand now. I am at my wits' end here, Lord. I despise life. I can't keep going like this. You say not to take meds — that You will be the one to get me out of this. But You're not. You haven't. Do You like to see me suffer? Do You like watching me in despair and watching me lose my mind? It's like You want to withhold the healing I need, yet You won't let me have the world's solution either — to be medicated into feeling better. But how do You benefit from me feeling such despair? I HATE THIS. I hate feeling like this and like I did last night where all I want is to curl up and die. If this were as easy as changing my attitude, I think that could have worked by now. Are You just sitting up there watching? What are You doing to me? I understand now more than ever why people leave suicide notes and give up. This world holds so much hopelessness and pain. You, Lord, are the only One with the power to change it. There is absolutely nothing I can do to fix anything in my life. If there was, believe me! I would have done it a hundred times over by now. I feel powerless to a powerful God who sits back and chooses to just watch me in this state.

God's reply: Stop fighting and let Me take over. Surrender. Make Me enough, and I will fill you. I don't want to overwhelm you before you're ready. There will come a day this experience will matter. It will be used. I will redeem this time. Just wait. It will make sense. I am the Rewarder of those who seek Me. Seek Me with all your heart, mind, and soul. There's no need for you to wander. Stay straight on My narrow path. I am Your Father. I sustain you. I number your days. I lay out the path for you. You just need to walk it. I've placed before you exactly what I want you to have. No more and no less. Time will unfold more blessings. This is just a season to be endured. You'll reach the other side of this. You'll be stronger. I am strengthening you daily. I'm carving you into who I want you to be.

January 23, 2004:

(The Lord spoke to a friend of mine while she was praying for me. This is her dialoguing with God, which strikingly matches mine. I had not shared with her anything God had told me when she had this conversation with God:)

God's reply: Trust Me with Cheryl. I am doing a work that surpasses your understanding as well as her own. I am her Physician. This has been a painful time for her, but it has been necessary for her growth and maturity in Me. I am giving her the opportunity to grow up in Me, and those growing pains are derailing her. In a while, she will find firmer footing in her commitment to Me. She is disappointed in Me now; but I assure you, everything that I have allowed has been for her growth and for her good. Do I not take the time to do what is best, no matter the cost? I am patient, even to watch as My children suffer if I know it is for their good. There is much more at stake than you realize. Cheryl is at a crossroads. She is deciding whether it is worth it to serve Me. Her anger will fade, though, and I will be waiting, knowing that she will love Me fully again. She will make no progress until this happens. As long as she is in this place, I will wait; but I will not move on with her until we are again in right relationship.

(My friend then addressed the issue with God about how I felt that trusting and surrendering to God is what got me into this mess to begin with.)

God's reply: She trusted me, but she did not surrender. She trusted that I would work things out according to her desires. That is not surrender. What I have asked of her is excruciating, but it is also essential. At the same time, when she looks back, years from now, it will feel like a moment, a distant memory. She has resisted this growth, but I know it is right for her. There is much I have ahead for her if only she will allow Me to do it. Fear disables her. I understand her desire to know that she has some things that are constants. I want her to find that in Me, and I will suffer with her through this difficulty until she does.

(The accuracy with which this friend heard from God amazed me. God told her my exact feelings, words I wrote privately in my journal, like how I was at a crossroads, trying to figure out if I wanted to still follow Him. You can review that entry in Chapter 11. God also told her many of the same things He'd been trying to get through to me and my stubborn head. God even told me the same thing about how one day this pain would be a faded memory and reminded me He wanted my surrender. If anything, God is the same yesterday, today, and forever. And the same Heavenly Father who speaks to my friends speaks to me. This was yet another way He confirmed for me I had been communing with my God. It woke me up to His goodness and presence.)

February 01, 2004:

Cheryl's prayer: Lord, I'm back in Your court, not wanting to work against You anymore. Not wanting to fight anymore. Circumstances have not changed. I don't see any changes ahead, but I feel better. And that's where I believe You want me to be. And I mean it, which is the most important thing.

God's reply: I always welcome you back with open arms. You are My child, through and through. You are never far away, even when you push. You will stand in awe as you watch My ways at work in your life. You will know undoubtedly it is Me at work. Your despair is ending. It is a season that is about to be over. You can rejoice in My mercy and love. Times are changing, and it will all come anew. I have been placing the pieces. Follow the leading of My hands, the rhythm I set. Rest in My peace. It is yours. I love you, My precious child.

February 02, 2004:

Cheryl's prayer: Lord, is there anything you'd like to say to me today?

God's reply: Cheryl, I love you and I'm pouring out My grace upon you, so you can pour My grace upon others. Take this season. Work on your book. The success story will come. And it will be My success, My healing bestowed upon you.

Cheryl's prayer: Lord, please keep speaking to me. I know it's what is lifting this depression.

God's reply: I will. It pleases Me that you want to hear from Me. I am your Wonderful Counselor. I can speak words of comfort directly to your heart. I can weed out bitterness. I can take care of that when you surrender it to Me. We are doing a beautiful work in your heart! It will all make sense, the pain and anguish. Just like My pain and anguish make perfect sense. There is always a reason. I take care of you, and I've taken care of your heart and your roads ahead. Walk the roads with Me. I will not lead you astray or down the wrong pathways. My ways are right. My ways are best for you.

February 10, 2004:

Cheryl's prayer: Lord, is there anything you'd like to say to me today?

God's reply: My tender Cheryl, let Me love you for a while. Make Me enough. Your love is coming. He is coming. Put it aside for now and wait on Me. You will watch My faithfulness unfold. You have plenty to focus on right now. It will sneak up on you when you least expect it. Lay it all down. I have given you plenty of tasks. Focus on those. Let Me pave the way for your love story. You don't need to do anything. Let Me write your love story. Let Me be the author.

APPENDIX B
12-Step Method:
Pulling it All Together

This is a twelve-step method, summarizing the main steps outlined in this book, to give you a place to start your journey toward recovery. Feel free to modify any step to fit your particular situation.

1. Admit to yourself that you have a problem. Give up trying to be perfect and admit that anxiety is a problem you need to handle. Left unattended, it grows.

2. *Believe* that God can help you recover. *Believe* He can restore you. (If necessary, do a biblical research project to explore His healing ways and the peace He offers if we'll pursue it. Read about this until you truly believe it!)

3. Go to God, admit that you need His help, and accept His guidance. Turn your will over to God. Stop trying to do it alone. Surrender.

4. Admit your problem to others: friends, family. Stop hiding your problem. Learn to stop showing others a false image of perfection.

5. Go to counseling or support groups. Find others trained to help with your particular problem or others who understand what you're going through.

6. Take an inventory of your past and present. Read old journal entries. Ask God to help you identify moments from your past that may have contributed to the problem. Ask God to help you remember only what you need to remember. Deal with those memories, under the guidance of a professional counselor if needed. Then be willing to put them behind you.

7. Creatively work through your disorder. Journal regularly. Ask yourself probing questions. Explore all areas of the past. Record panics, symptoms, victories, goals, steps taken, your reaction to symptoms. Figure out what beliefs you hold that may be harmful. Journal about lies you tell yourself in your mind, then explore the Bible for the truth or ask God to rewrite them. Memorize verses that combat the lies, so you can recite them to yourself during a moment of panic. Write out your feelings in creative forms. (Scripts, stories, poems, songs.)

8. Learn all the coping techniques that aid you during panic attacks. Learn relaxation and breathing exercises. Practice stopping the stream of lies that go through your mind and replace those thoughts with God's truths. Create your coping cards of encouraging verses, relaxation instructions and anything else that may be helpful to you during a moment of panic.

9. Research, read, and learn. Knowledge is definitely power. There are always new books, techniques, and testimonies online or in books.

10. See a doctor to rule out any possible physical problems. Get a diagnosis so you can be certain it is a panic or anxiety disorder that you have. (A counselor or psychiatrist can give you a written evaluation.) Find out if medication is necessary.

11. Work on your relationship with God. Learn to trust Him. Have a daily fellowship with Him. Take walks with God. Read, pray, listen. Learn how to hear His voice, His leading. Learn to listen to God through the many ways He speaks: His still small voice, His Word, dreams, and vision. Let God be your Counselor.

12. Reach out to help others just like you. It can bring value to your suffering. Share anything helpful you learn with others.

CHAPTER NOTES

Introduction
   1. Anxiety Disorders Association of America

Chapter 1
   1. Malcolm Smith. *Freedom From Fear.* (TX: Malcolm Smith Ministries), p. 14.
   2. Mark & Patti Virkler, *Prayers that Heal the Heart* (FL: Bridge-Logos Publishers, 2001), Introduction page.
   3. Mark & Patti Virkler, *Prayers that Heal the Heart* Seminar Guide (NY: Communion With God Ministries, 2000), p. 3–4.
   4. Mark & Patti Virkler, *Counseled by God.* (NY: Lamad Publishing, 2002), p. 65.

Chapter 2
   1. Agnes, Michael, Editor in Chief. *Webster's New World College Dictionary.* (CA: IDG Books Worldwide, Inc., 2000, 4th edition). p. 64, 1040.
   2. Archibald D. Hart, Ph.D. *Overcoming Anxiety* (TX: Word Publishing, 1989), p. 69–70.
   3. Mark & Patti Virkler, *Counseled by God.* (NY: Lamad Publishing, 2002), p. 61, 63, 69.

Chapter 3
   1. Archibald D. Hart, Ph.D. *Overcoming Anxiety* (TX: Word Publishing, 1989), p. 7.
   2. Malcolm Smith. *Freedom from Fear* (TX: Malcolm Smith Ministries, 1993), p. 35.

Chapter 4
1. Christa Sands. *Learning to Trust Again* (MI: Discovery House Publishers, 1999), p.46, 199, 76.
2. Archibald D. Hart, Ph.D. *Overcoming Anxiety* (TX: Word Publishing, 1989), p. 17–18, 157.

Chapter 6
1. Christa Sands. *Learning to Trust Again* (MI: Discovery House Publishers, 1999), p. 30, 44, 42.
2. Ibid., p. 21.

Chapter 9
1. Malcolm Smith. *Freedom from Fear* (TX: Malcolm Smith Ministries, 1993), p. 24.
2. Herman Riffel. *Dream Interpretation: A Biblical Understanding* (PA: Destiny Image, 1993), p. 20, 89.

Chapter 10
1. Malcolm Smith. *Freedom from Fear* (TX: Malcolm Smith Ministries, 1993), p. 38–39, 46.
2. Mark & Patti Virkler. *Prayers that Heal the Heart* (FL: Bridge-Logos Publishers, 2001), p.57–58.
3. Ibid., p. 60.
4. Frank & Ida Mae Hammond. *Pigs in the Parlor.* (MO: Impact Christian Books, 1973). Pg. 5–7.

Chapter 11
1. Mark & Patti Virkler, *Counseled by God.* (NY: Lamad Publishing, 2002), p. 106.
2. Mark & Patti Virkler, *Prayers that Heal the Heart* (FL: Bridge-Logos Publishers, 2001), p. 64.

ACKNOWLEDGMENTS

This book would not be complete without thanking all the people who helped me get where I am today. To them, I owe much gratitude.

To my parents, whose support for me and for this project has touched my heart. My sister, Heather and her wonderful family, my aunt, Jackie, whose support means more to me than you could ever know, and my late grandmother, Marcelle.

To the treasures in my life, my friends and mentors, Susan and Connie, who counseled me through the most difficult seasons of my life. To our Women's Prayer Group—all of you are beautiful, and you are amazing gifts from God to me.

Additionally, I'd like to thank Lisa, whose friendship is never ending. To Bart, Caroline, Deanna, Donna, Jason, Shannon, Lana, Marilyn & Phil, Laura, JoAnna, Kristi, Rene, Jessica, and everyone else who had an impact on this area of my life. To the awesome Brooks and Price families.

My gratitude to Peggy, for her wise counsel and editorial advice on this manuscript.

And to Karla: you made a huge difference and you don't even realize it. And the same goes for "Amy" and "Matty."

A very special thank you to Lisa Crates, who got to be with Chris and me, photographing our engagement through our wedding day. (She took the photo we used on the cover of this book.)

Thank you to Michael English, whose bravery in speaking out about his panic disorder started me on my road toward recovery (and to Sheila Walsh, whose interview of Michael on *Heart to Heart with Sheila Walsh* unlocked so much for me).

I offer many blessings to Mark & Patti Virkler of Communion with God Ministries, and Christian Leadership University for all they've taught me, as well as my professor and mentor, from CLU, Karen King. And their daughter, Charity, whose support means so much to me.

And thanks to all who allowed me to quote your material, especially Christa Sands, whose book had a big impact on me.

Naturally, I hold a special place in my heart for those I dated, whose impact on me is relayed in this book. To protect their privacy I changed all of their names.

To Chris. You are such an amazing and healing presence in my life. God couldn't have picked a more calming presence for me either. I'm so glad to be on this journey with you.

And lastly, to my Lord and Savior, Jesus Christ, who saved me, who loves me and who gave me His Holy Spirit to do this amazing work. I am your bride, first and foremost. It is with joy I eagerly await Your return for me.

ABOUT THE AUTHOR

Cheryl McKay has been professionally writing since 1997. Cheryl wrote the screenplay for *The Ultimate Gift*, based on Jim Stovall's novel. The award-winning film stars James Garner, Brian Dennehy, and Abigail Breslin and was released in theaters by Fox in 2007. *The Ultimate Gift* won a Crystal Heart Award at the Heartland Film Festival, received three Movieguide Nominations, winning one of the Ten Best Family Films of 2007, and won a CAMIE Award, for one of the Top Ten Films of the year. Cheryl also wrote the DVD for *Gigi: God's Little Princess*, another book adaptation based on the book by Sheila Walsh, as well as the *Wild and Wacky, Totally True Bible Stories* audio series and books with Frank Peretti. She wrote a half hour drama for teenagers about high school violence, called *Taylor's Wall*. It was produced in Los Angeles by Family Theater Productions. McKay wrote a script called *Greetings from the Flipside*, commissioned by Art Within, after winning a year-long fellowship. It's being novelized for B&H Publishing with Rene Gutteridge. Her screenplay, *Never the Bride*, has been adapted into a novel for Random House Publishers and was released in June 2009. It won Best Women's Fiction book at the Carol Awards/Book of the Year Awards at ACFW and was a finalist in the top three Women's Fiction books at the Inspirational Reader's Choice Awards. She wrote the screen story for *The Ultimate Life*. And she released *Finally the Bride: Finding Hope While Waiting*, a book for singles losing hope while waiting to find love.

Photo Credit: Vincent Wallace / Silver Hill Images

Visit Cheryl's Website at:

www.purplepenworks.com

Visit Cheryl's Blog at:

www.finallyone.com

Visit Cheryl's Twitter: @PurplePenWorks

From the screenwriter of
The Ultimate Gift & Never the Bride

Finally
Fearless
Workbook

Journey from
Panic to Peace

Cheryl McKay

Get the workbook that accompanies this book. The *Finally Fearless Workbook* is a great tool for church groups, book clubs, or individuals who want to play an active role in their healing from fear and anxiety.

From the Back Cover of the *Finally Fearless Workbook*:

From Cheryl's Journal:
Why am I like this? What is wrong with me? Why am I so afraid? I can't
control my anxiety; these fears seem to overtake me. Does anyone know how I
feel? No one else has this problem. I am a freak, and I am alone. Where is God
in this?

Do fear and anxiety rule your life?

They used to rule mine.

I am not a medical doctor or a psychologist. I am a creative, intelligent woman. Yet panic and anxiety left me feeling completely out of control. I ached for God to show up and heal me instantly. Instead, He became my Wonderful Counselor, and He walked me through my fears, step by step, toward healing.

Much of my personal recovery came through healing exercises I did, the same ones I'm now sharing with you in this companion workbook. The work you will do here is a reflection of God's relentless help in healing and encouraging me through these most vital exercises, creative assignments, journaling, reflection, and meditation on key scriptures.

This workbook also contains bonus material not found in the original book, including extra journal entries, assignments, poetry, and helpful collections of Bible verses grouped by topics like peace, hope, God's faithfulness, fear, and trust.

Are you tired of fighting against your fears? Has panic interrupted your life? Has anxiety stopped you from going after your dreams? Start your soul-searching journey now so you, too, can venture toward peace.

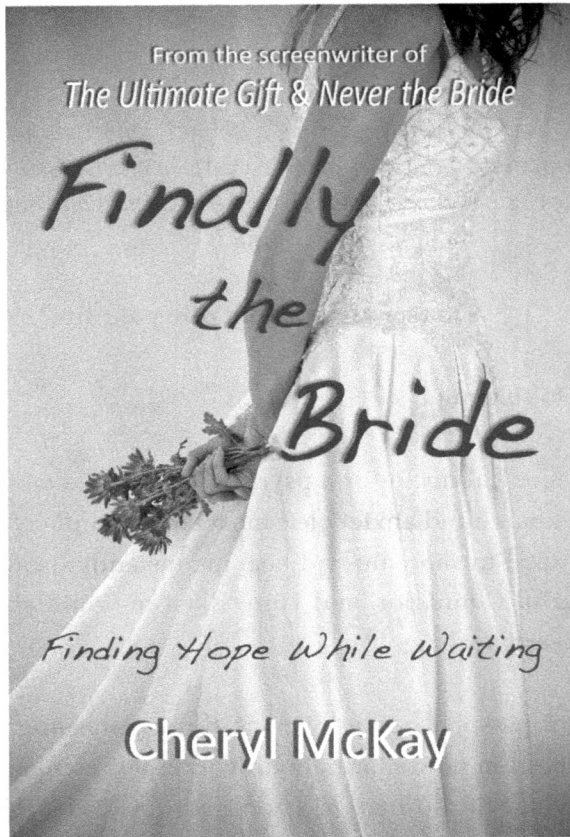

From the screenwriter of
The Ultimate Gift & *Never the Bride*

Finally the Bride

Finding Hope While Waiting

Cheryl McKay

From the Back Cover of *Finally the Bride: Finding Hope While Waiting*:

Why Would God Care About My Love Life?

From the woman behind the screenplay and novel, *Never the Bride*, comes a roller coaster of a love story with God. Cheryl McKay pulls no punches about what it's really like to be single, with your age creeping up, and no end in sight to the wait for love and marriage. It seems that many years ago, God asked Cheryl to surrender the pen she was using to write her love story. All He wanted was carte blanche. No problem, right?

Cheryl tentatively conceded—that is, until it became apparent that the Almighty had no intention of conforming to her writing schedule, much less the tick of her biological clock. In fact, He blew every deadline she ever attempted to set. As romance seemed to pass Cheryl by, she couldn't help but question: Could God really be trusted to bring her the love of her life?

Written during a long wait, this book opens up Cheryl's painfully honest, personal journals. She explores what it's like to enlist in God's Marriage Boot Camp, and how to survive singlehood year after solitary year. She wrestles with her Creator over multiple best friends that never see her "that way." Then there are those lists of what she wanted—you know, the ones she revised a billion times then laminated for safekeeping. She watches, bewildered, as much younger women find love that seems to elude her.

Through it all, she falls head over heels for a God who proves Himself to be as resistant to her controls as He is faithful beyond her wildest dreams. Are you still waiting? Have you lost hope? Venture to victory with a woman who knows just how hard it is to wait for the day when you are *Finally the Bride*.

This book includes a collection of real-life, God-written love stories by such authors as SQuire Rushnell & Louise DuArt (*God Winks Series, Couples Who Pray*), and Victorya Michaels Rogers (*Finding a Man Worth Keeping*).

never
the
bride

a novel

cheryl mckay
& rene gutteridge

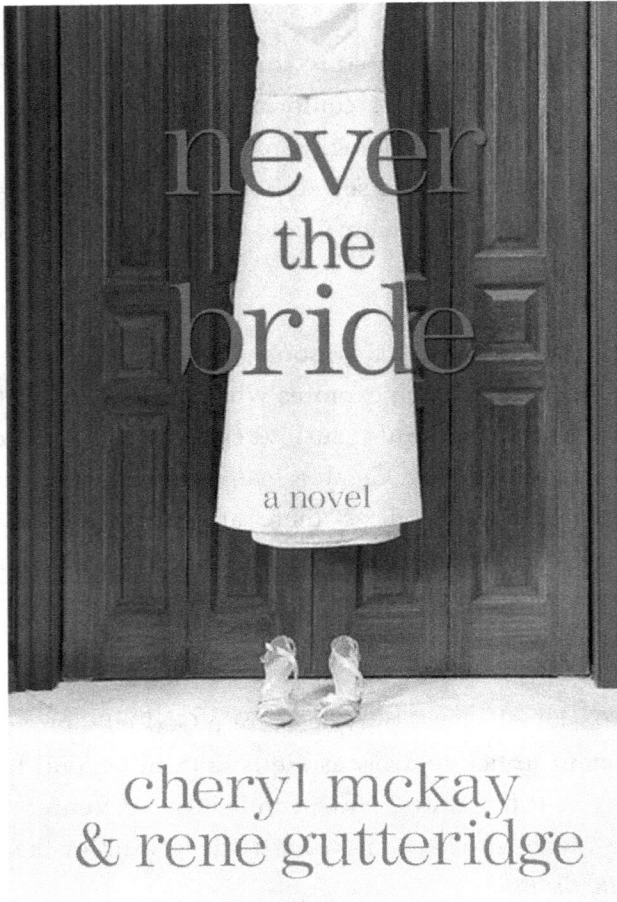

NEVER THE BRIDE a novel by Cheryl McKay & Rene Gutteridge
Published by Waterbrook Press

SUGGESTED READING LIST

Backus, Nathan & Chapian, Marie, *Telling Yourself the Truth* (MN: Bethany House Publishers, 1980).

Bennett, Rita, *You Can Be... Emotionally Free* (FL: Bridge-Logos Publishers, 1982).

Bourne, Ph.D., Edmund J., *The Anxiety & Phobia Workbook* (CA: New Harbinger Publications, Inc., 1990).

Curtis, Brent & Eldredge, John, *The Sacred Romance* (TN: Thomas Nelson Publishers, 1997).

Eldredge, John, *Journey of Desire* (TN: Thomas Nelson Publishers, 1997).

Hammond, Frank & Ida Mae, *Pigs in the Parlor.* (MO: Impact Christian Books, 1973).

Hart, Ph.D., Archibald D., *Overcoming Anxiety* (TX: Word Publishing, 1989).

Hill, Craig, *Ancient Paths* (CO: Family Foundations Publishing, 1992).

Meyer, Joyce, *Battlefield of the Mind* (OK: Harrison House, 1995).

Peretti, Frank, *The Wounded Spirit* (TN: Word Publishing, 2000).

Prince, Derek, *Blessing or Curse: You Can Choose* (MI: Chosen Books, 2000).

Rohrer, Susan, *The Holy Spirit: Amazing Power for Everyday People* (Amazon Digital Publishing, 2011).

Riffel, Herman, *Dream Interpretation: A Biblical Understanding* (PA: Destiny Image, 1993).

Sands, Christa, *Learning to Trust Again* (MI: Discovery House Publishers, 1999).

Sorge, Bob, *Pain, Perplexity and Promotion* (MO: Oasis House, 1999).

Sorge, Bob, *The Fire of Delayed Answers* (MO: Oasis House, 1996).

Smith, Malcolm, *Freedom from Fear* (TX: Malcolm Smith Ministries, 1993).

Smith, Malcolm, *Searching for Self—Worth* (TX: Malcolm Smith Ministries).

Thomas, Benny, *Exploring the World of Dreams* (PA: Whitaker House, 1990).

Virkler, Mark & Patti, *Prayers that Heal the Heart* (FL: Bridge-Logos Publishers, 2001).

Virkler, Mark & Patti, *Dialogue with God* (FL: Bridge-Logos Publishers, 1986). (Updated as *4 Keys to Hearing God's Voice*, Destiny Image, 2010).

Virkler, Mark & Patti, *Communion with God* (PA: Destiny Image, 1995).

Virkler, Mark & Patti, *Counseled by God* (NY: Lamad Publishing, 2002).

Virkler, Mark & Patti, *Counseled by God Workbook.* (NY: Communion With God Ministries, 1986).

Walsh, Sheila, *Living Fearlessly* (MI: Zondervan Publishing House, 2001).

Wilson, Ph.D., R. Reid, *Don't Panic* (NY: Harper Perennial, 1986).

www.ingramcontent.com/pod-product-compliance
Lightning Source LLC
Chambersburg PA
CBHW060839280326
41934CB00007B/842